Dear Mom and Dad
(An Adventure in Obedience)

R. R. Smith

Introduction

Why am I writing a book? It feels presumptuous. "Here, read a book about our lives." My only recourse is to pray that these words will point to God and bring Him glory. We serve an amazing God, a God who is able to use anything for His glory, even our family's story. It's time to give Him the credit He is due.

My husband and I lived in India for 12 years. The cities are crowded and dirty. Travel is difficult. We were ill often. Even so, we would not trade our time there for anything. It's not just that living there changed us. It did, but God forbid that our personal growth would be the only reason. Mostly, we loved our front row seats to His show. We witnessed miracles we never imagined we'd see, and saw Him save the lost in great numbers.

We weren't the type who'd prayed for India years, or longed to visit. I'd not read Amy Carmichael's writings, nor did I have a positive opinion about William Cary. We never sponsored an Indian child through one of those ministries, had no longing to see the Taj Mahal. How did our family end up living in that ancient land?

I have always loved *going*. Family history, parental choices, and life circumstances fueled my love. When I was 12, I already knew what I wanted to do with my life - be a teacher of missionary children overseas. To that end, I eventually attended a college which allowed the education majors to complete their practice teaching in other countries. I couldn't wait to *go*.

Three years after graduation, I met Steve. When we began dating seriously, we often discussed my desire to go. He was passionate about making my dream come true. In October of 1996 we married, knowing that at some point we would live outside of the United States.

Sometimes, I tried to guess where we might go. I worried. How would God find a place for a teacher and an engineer? We refused to believe that God had made us one through marriage only to call us to different types of work. So, we waited. We wondered. We prayed.

Finally, the answer came. In the Spring of 2000 we heard about a Christian, non-profit organization for engineers and architects. They had an opening in their India office, an opportunity too "tailor made" to ignore. Steve could use his engineering skills. I could help mentor the college-aged interns. That Fall, we took our "scouting trip." Steve left first. He helped with a project in central India for two weeks, then I, with our 18-month old daughter, joined him. The three of us traveled up into the Himalayan foothills to see the office and meet the staff.

Here I sit, 17 years after we visited the subcontinent for the first time. It's hard to remember how I felt. I know how I feel now, but how did I feel back when we were living the opening paragraph of this chapter of our lives? Below is an excerpt from the letter we mailed to our friends and family shortly after our return:

Dec. 2000

...the poverty was shocking. And there were lots of rules: don't drink the water, don't rinse off your toothbrush in the sink, walk right past the monkeys and cows in the roads. Through it all, we felt God's grace, as if every road we walked were paved with it. I'd been nervous about morning sickness with Baby #2. Hardly felt it. We had also worried about Eirene. Would she fly well? Would she eat well? Yes, emphatically, yes! Thank you for your prayers. She loved flying. She marched the aisles for exercise, watched people, slept hard, and warmed the heart of every flight attendant between here and India. Did she eat? She loved the food! The spicier the curry, the more she ate. Fried okra, lentils, cauliflower, chickpeas, she ate it all. We can't get her to eat hamburgers here the way she ate over there. India would have been boring without Eirene.

We feel the Lord calling us to commit 1-2 years of our lives to helping Indian church leaders realize their dreams. We're excited! And dazed. A year ago, we never would have dreamed our lives would be heading this direction. All we can say is, Thank You, Lord.

Excited. Dazed. I remember now. The crowds didn't bother me that first trip. Soon enough, they would. That trip drew Steve and me closer together. Later, we felt the adventure threaten to tear us apart. We were excited about using our gifts for God. Later, we would learn that life isn't about us or our talents, but about God and His abilities.

When we boarded the plane one year later, there were four of us. Baby Isabel was four months old. Eirene was 2 1/2 years. How to explain the concept of goodbye to a toddler? How to keep from sobbing through final moments with family and dear friends? Going was harder than we'd ever imagined. Some family we never saw again.

God is worth every discomfort and the stretch of every heart string. We pray that through the reading of these pages, you will come to agree.

R.R. Smith,
December 2017

I am the true grapevine,
and my Father is the gardener...
*He **prunes** the branches*
that do bear fruit
so they will produce
***even more**....*
Those who remain in me,
and I in them,
*will produce **much** fruit...*
Apart from me
you can do nothing.
*When you produce **much** fruit,*
you are my
*true **disciples**...*
(John 15:1-8)

September 2001 - December 2006

Pruning

Pruning? Not really. More like
hacking a path through the jungle
with a machete.

Can you remember when trips to the airport included long goodbyes (or kiss-filled hellos) at the gate? Never again. Nine days after we left America, planes were hijacked, and thousands died in the attacks of 9/11.

We wrote an email to our loved ones soon after our arrival, but due to internet difficulties the email didn't actually send until September 11. That is, it was September 11 on our side of the world. In America, it was still September 10, and the events of the next day had yet to be suffered.

We do not see the timing of our departure as accidental. Throughout the summer of 2001, we considered and re-considered the date. Should we leave as soon as possible, or should we give ourselves a little cushion between preparing and departure? What was the right thing to do? I still cannot explain it, but my opinion never wavered during our discussions - we were to aim for August, Labor Day weekend at the latest. I didn't know why. No one ever suggested that timing to me, and no one would have begrudged us a little rest period once all the details were finalized.

We see God's hand in the timing of our departure. What if we had allowed ourselves a week or two of buffer before leaving for India? Only the Father knows.

11 September 2001
Dear Mom and Dad,

We made it. We are here on a mountain covered with fog. The monsoon is still here, the mist still hiding the highest peaks from view. How good it is to be here!

It is now 3:30 in the afternoon which means it is 4:00 am in Austin. We left Texas 5 days ago. Thank you for your prayers. We have felt His amazing, sustaining grace throughout these days.

The trip went well. Eirene was so excited that she didn't need our help staying entertained during the first flight. On the second leg, we decided to see if she'd sleep. Just like at home, we put her pajamas on. Read a book. Said prayers and sang *Jesus loves me*. We were seated in the first row of economy, so had extra leg room. We made a little place for her to sleep right there on the floor, and wouldn't you know it, she put her head on her pillow and went to sleep! She slept the whole flight. We woke her about 30 minutes outside of Amsterdam.

When we finally arrived Delhi, we still had a 24-hour wait for the train, then a seven hour train ride, finally a 90-minute taxi, and now here we are, on the other side of the world. Our new home.

We've spent most of the day unpacking, trying to keep ourselves awake in order to adjust to the time difference as quickly as possible. The first night in Delhi, we fell asleep about 9:00 pm, but then all woke about 1:30 in the morning. Eirene began jumping on the bed, shouting, "All finished bed, Mama, all finished bed!" We spent the next two hours trying to convince her that since the sun was still in bed, we had to be, too. She finally fell back to sleep.

Now, we're trying to make this place feel like home, becoming acquainted with the four interns already here, and trying to explain to Eirene why we can't go to Gramma's house.

We're happy to be here. Overwhelmed. There's mold on everything. We spent most of the morning scrubbing bottles and plastic containers in our bathroom. Mold is growing on the front porch concrete and every tree. Something tells me I will never forget the smell of a house at the end of the monsoon season.

We know we'll be adjusting for a while, but we also know we're exactly where we're supposed to be. We miss you already (terribly), but we rejoice in God and are setting our hearts to worship Him, no matter the place, our mood, or even (these days) the time of day!

Hey, look who just woke up from her nap. Isabel fell asleep at the start of this email, and now Eirene is waking at the end of it. Toddler bedhead is cute.

We love you,
Robin, for us all

16 September 2001

Dear Mom and Dad,

It was good to talk with you this morning, to hear your voices, and to hear how God is using this horrible tragedy to His good purposes. That's been our prayer, that God would use the attack on New York City to draw His Body together.

I keep thinking about the Crusades, and how we Believers were the ones who perpetrated horrible attacks against people who didn't believe in Christ. Anyone can stoop low - even Christians - when physical domination and power are the objectives. Philip Yancey writes about the temptation of power. Throughout history, whenever the Church has been a powerful institution, she has become corrupt and tyrannical. Lord, don't let us gain places of power! May we choose the way of Your cross.

It's Saturday afternoon. We just returned from a picnic at the Company Garden, a public garden the British built over 100 years ago. It was good to spend time with our new co-workers, but then, just as we were about to hike a hill up to an old castle, it was *draw a line in the sand* time with Eirene.

These "hills" are the foothills of the tallest mountains in the world. We easily descend or ascend 500 feet during a 10-minute walk. The trails have such tight switchbacks that from the air they look like the letter Z. A few days ago, we were walking home from the hospital. Eirene got so tired that she couldn't go on.

"OK," I said, "then I'll carry you. Here, get on my back."

Then, oh my, you've never seen such a fight! She just refused to ride piggyback! Cried. Yelled. Stamped her feet. Maybe she was scared? We weren't sure, but since we were hot, tired and hungry, we decided it wasn't the time to fight the battle, and just picked her up and carried her.

So there we were today, ready to hike another steep mountain trail. I offered to carry her on my back.

"No!"

She kicked and screamed. We tried to reason with her, but she just threw herself on the ground and wailed. She's too heavy for me to carry in my arms. Piggyback is a must. This was the moment.

"Eirene, you're going to ride on Mama's back. Yes...You are going to ride on Mama's back, and you're going to be content. Stop crying. Here we go!"

I put her on my back. Kept my voice happy, "Yay! When Mama was little, Mama rode on Grandpa Steve's back. No, stop crying, Eirene. Here we go!"

And so it went. We walked, stopped, then started again. When we finally reached the top, she scampered off to play around the castle, happy as anything.

When it was time to leave, I said, "Eirene, we're going to walk back down to the car, now, and you're going to ride on Dad's back. Yes, Mom?"

She said, "Yes, Mom," and that was it.

Steve picked her up, put her on his back, and a few minutes later she declared, "I like piggy back!"

Just a little levity during this time of mourning. Know that we do mourn with you, even from the other side of the world.

Love,
Robin, for all

22 September 2001

Dear Mom and Dad,

Yesterday, the girls and I were invited to a playdate. The mom said that she lives close to our house, and since Eirene didn't mind being the only girl ("Play with kids, Mama!"), I gladly accepted the invitation. Isabel rode in the baby carrier on my chest, I slung the bag of baby supplies over my shoulder, took Eirene by the hand, and off we went! In literature, this is called foreshadowing.

There are streets in our town, but it's generally faster to hike the narrow, steep paths instead of driving. Eirene is wondering where a good old fashioned car seat is when you want one. No such luck. In this town, we walk and pant and rest and then walk some more.

So, there we went, off to visit new friends. I knew the right path to take, but I wasn't sure how far down the mountain to go. The lady said they were about the 4th house down, but she couldn't exactly remember because, like us, they are also new. I figured, how hard could it be? We'll just walk until we hear kids. Right? By the time we passed the fourth house, I was exhausted. How many feet had we descended? 500? 600? I wasn't sure, but I knew that with each step down, the path back UP was going to be that much worse. Panicking, I finally decided enough was enough. We'd just have to try again another day. Poor Eirene.

When we turned around to start the climb back up, she wept. "I want to play with the boys! I'm so tired, Mama. Carry me, Mama." As we hiked, I kept talking in my calmest voice while Eirene cried in her loudest. I couldn't blame her, though. She was so disappointed. Coming back was hard. She's not even three years old. Thing is, the only way home was back up that mountain, and the only way up was to walk.

We walked and rested, and she cried and I wiped her nose, then we walked and rested while she cried. Finally, I carried her on my back. A couple of locals passed us. There we were: a sweaty white lady with a sleeping infant on her chest and a screaming toddler on her back, large bag hanging off one elbow. We finally made it back to the road where we sat for a few minutes to catch our breath. Thankfully, another new friend heard the crying and offered us a ride to our gate. She dropped us off 90 minutes after we'd begun, but we still weren't done. Eirene and I stared at the gate, all red faced and panting, then gazed UP at our house which sits (of course) on a hill above the road.

I looked at Eirene, and with sin in my heart, said, "You're going to walk up to the house by yourself."

Eirene started crying, and I, the missionary mama that I am, looked my 2 1/2 year old daughter in the eye and said (God, forgive me), "Stop crying, Eirene. You don't get to cry. Walk."

She did.

I apologized to her later. Am still ashamed about my horrible attitude. I am a sinner.

I love you and miss you,
Robin, for us all

29 September 2001

Dear Mom and Dad,

Eirene is napping, but Isabel is awake and lying on the floor right next to me. Everyone loves her. Every time I turn around a different person is holding her. She smiles all the time. She might speak Hindi before English.

Last night, as I was putting Eirene to bed, the last thing I told her was the last thing I say every night, "Jesus is with you here in your room, even when I can't be."

All of a sudden her eyes lit up, and she said, "Jesus, right here," and patted the pillow next to her.

I smiled and said, "Yes, Jesus is right next to you, and He's under you and above you, and all around you, and when you're ready, you can ask Him to come into your heart, and He'll open the door and come right in."

She sings an old Sunday School song about that, so after I mentioned Jesus opening the door, she said, "Behold! Knock, knock, open the door!"

I said, "That's right, Sweetie. One day you'll pray and Jesus will come right through that door."

She lay there, looking at me, so I thought, *Well, why not?* and I asked, "Eirene, would you like to ask Him to come in right now?"

She said, "Right now."

I said, "Then repeat after me, 'Jesus, come into my heart right now.' "

Sure enough, she said, "Jesus, come into my heart right now." Isn't that cool? I pushed it a little bit and said, "And make me into a new person," but she didn't repeat my words. She just looked at me and said, "No remember the words, Mama."

Isn't that amazing? She understood the first part, and quickly repeated it, but she wouldn't repeat the part she didn't understand. At least, that's how I see it.

Very cool. Our toddler is accepting Jesus as much as she can understand to.

Love you all,
Robin, for us all

28 October 2001
Dear Mom and Dad,

A current decision we're facing is about worship services: do we attend a Hindi service or an English one? When we arrived last month, we assumed that we'd join the only fully bi-lingual congregation in town, but began to doubt that assumption recently when we visited a Hindi service. Even through the language barrier, we felt the authenticity of the people. We also enjoyed participating in a service so different from what we're used to. We took off our shoes before entering the building, then sat cross-legged on mats on the floor. I wish I could discuss the options with you in person.

I wish I could discuss a lot of things with you. The one about Steve backing the jeep into our own gate is a good story, but so is the description of our recent anniversary dinner. We went over to the town's only five-star hotel for the buffet. All-you-can-eat buffet still only cost $5 per person, and that included entertainment - an Indian group playing Carpenters' tunes on the sitar!

We greatly miss you and love you dearly.
Robin, for us all

30 October 2001
Dear Mom and Dad,

Guess what? An actual package arrived in today's mail! Thank you! At first, I only stared at the box in confusion - *It's no one's birthday, why did my mom send us a package?* Then I opened it and saw the hat. I forgot you were going to make one for Isabel. Her bald head thanks you. It fits great. She's wearing it right now. She's coughing, too, so it seems the hat arrived just in time.

Yesterday, I took Eirene down to see the doctor. Steve was busy in the office. I left Isabel in the care of the house helper, and set off with Eirene for the hospital. She still isn't crazy about riding piggy back, so I was nervous about how things would go, but the Lord covered. He gave me the idea to tell stories while she rides my back. Goldilocks. The Little Red Hen. Cinderella. Those three got us down the hill. Took four stories to get us back up the hill, but it worked like a charm. Doctor diagnosed bronchitis and an ear infection. Please pray for us. I think the enemy is trying his hardest to get us discouraged and distracted by all this illness. It's kind of working.

I am learning that the washing of bodies requires much planning. There's a 10-gallon water tank attached to the wall in the bathroom. About 30 minutes before we want to bathe, we flip a switch and the water in the tank begins to heat. The timing can be tricky. If the water gets too hot, it boils and the steam build-up keeps it from flowing. No bath. Have to wait a few hours for it to cool down. On days when I've timed it correctly, I fill a bucket with hot water while filling another bucket with cold water at the sink. I then dump both buckets into the tub. Repeat. Then, I take a bath. There's not enough water to actually fill the tub, though. No restful soak in a bath of bubbles in this picture. This is all business. I miss showers.

I am also now the official Purchaser of Groceries for the house which includes all office staff, interns and our family. Every Monday morning, I call two different grocery stores to place our orders. The first store is the biggest grocery in town, which means it's about the size of a 7-Eleven. The smaller store is the size of a nice walk-in closet. No joke. Amazing how much produce they have packed in there. The store owners spend the day packing our order into trunks, then they hire coolies to carry the trunks to our house. Coolies are men who carry anything on their backs - even refrigerators - up and down these trails. On their backs. I don't know how they do it. They're little people, these guys, but carrying goods is how they make a living. Lucky ones earn about $2 a day. Our house is located about 900 feet above, and a little over a mile away from the stores. Every Monday evening, here they come in their flip-flops, our food on their backs. We always try to give them what's considered a good tip, about 45 cents US. Unbelievable. Back home, that's the price of a pack of gum. What do I do with this disparity, Lord? Help us.

That's a glimpse into my world.

Thanks, again, for the love-filled hat!

Love you both,
Robin, for us all

21 November 2001

Happy Thanksgiving, Mom and Dad!

Our lives are full of sounds. I wish you could hear them. They are new sounds that we never heard back in Austin.

In the morning, first thing, there's the sound of rushing water - music to our ears. Back home people pay money for recordings of this, right? Here, we have the city fathers to thank. It means that the city has water that day, and some of it has made its way through the pipes to fill the tanks perched on our metal roof. This sound brings relief because it means we can bathe that day, wash dishes, even do a load of laundry. However, on some mornings, we check our watches all of a sudden and realize it's already after 7:00 and we haven't heard the rushing waters. On those mornings, Steve climbs the ladder to the roof, to check the tanks, always hoping that maybe we just didn't hear it. Usually, he sees that, no, it didn't come. On those days, we eat on paper plates, do no laundry, flush toilets only when absolutely necessary, and buy drinking water from the store down the road. Oh my, but we love the sound of rushing water.

After the swoosh of water come the footsteps on the roof. Lumbering, stomping footsteps. Sometimes running fast, sometimes slow and methodical. Monkeys! Every morning.

Tall pine trees surround our house. The monkeys swing down from the trees onto the patio, and then ascend the same ladder Steve uses to check the water tanks. Some mornings, they run because the dog is on the patio, barking furiously. Other mornings, when the dog is inside, the monkeys take their time. They are gray, and stand about three feet high. Some are mamas with babies. Eirene loves to watch them through the windows. She points, and says in a voice of wonder, "I saw a monkey!"

Then, at 9:00, another new morning sound. It is the house-help arriving, two women and one man. They enter the side door by the kitchen. The women hang their shawls on the hook, and then the three of them come to find us to wish us a good morning, in the Indian manner, of course. They put their palms together in front of their faces, bow their heads slightly, and say, "Namaste." Then, yet another new thing - the sound of Eirene responding. She puts her palms together, smiles broadly, and says, "Namaste." These are quickly becoming lovingly familiar sounds.

There's one more sound we wish you could hear - Isabel's laugh. She has a great laugh. She laughs when we rub her belly with our chins, but no one makes her laugh like Eirene. Isabel watches her big sister's every move, and when something strikes her, she laughs. Guffaws, really, which of course makes the rest of us laugh. You'd also enjoy hearing her start worship during Sunday services, too. We all stand, and in that quiet moment before the band starts to play, she lets out one of her happy squeaks, and then we know it's time to begin!

Sounds. So many permeate our lives here. Cows moo on the road below the house. The generator roars to life when the electricity goes out, more often than you can imagine. Eirene carries on long conversations with us during dinner. Isabel cries at 2:00 am as she is still learning to sleep through the night. Steve groans as he takes his bucket bath and the water isn't as warm as he'd like. Meanwhile, I try to speak Hindi (a new sound) with the house help while pointing, laughing and pantomiming to make my meaning clear.

On another note, thank you so much for praying for us and the girls since we wrote you last month. It was terrible seeing the girls that sick. Before moving here, I never pictured spending a night in a missionary hospital with an infant and a toddler suffering from pneumonia. Thankfully, God knew. He was with us there. We felt His grace. Also, we became better friends with the two missionary doctors. They are wonderful. We couldn't ask for better care for our girls. Again, God's grace.

And now, here we are in the midst of Thanksgiving preparations. We heard that there is a man in a nearby town who raises turkeys, so we ordered three. I can hear you from here: "Three?!!?" From what we've heard, these birds probably aren't turkeys, but rather small guinea hens, so who knows? Always an adventure, right? Most importantly, we'll be together, we'll be warm sitting next to the wood-burning stove, and we'll celebrate God's goodness in this place. We'll remember that the God who took care of the Pilgrims all those years ago hasn't changed. He's still in the business of taking care of His children, no matter how far from home they travel.

Happy Thanksgiving to you. We thank God for you. We love you.
Robin, for us all

15 December 2001
Dear Mom and Dad,

We're so looking forward to your visit! Truly, we are counting the days.

December has been the prettiest month thus far. We wake each morning to the view of the awesome, majestic Himalayas, ridge after ridge that seem to go on forever. That God is more immovable than a mountain is too awesome to comprehend.

In the past few days, the weather has turned cold and rainy. We're trying to spend as much time as possible in the living room with the *buchari* (pronounced boo-kar-ee, and is Hindi for wood burning stove). A *buchar* is a fever, so a buchari is an object that gives off a fever. Pretty cute. Anyway, we have all fallen in love with that large tin can. Though Steve has become adept at lighting it, we are all, unfortunately, accustomed to the smoke smell in the house. Bucharis are not known for their efficiency.

We met an interesting person recently. He is a follower of Christ. He used to have a secure job pastoring for a denominational church. He and his family lived in the comfortable parsonage. He owned a scooter. About five years ago, even though he wasn't sure why, he began to feel in his heart that it was time to do something else. He resigned his post. Prayed for guidance. Told the Lord that he needed a home for his family (they could no longer live in the parsonage), and he needed a ministry. He prayed with friends at 5:00 am everyday for two months. Finally, a group of people approached him about a village nearby that had an empty schoolhouse. Would he be interested in running a Christian school for those children? Then came more good news. Shortly after he started his new position, he and his family were invited to live rent free in a house for one year. Then, someone else pledged to buy food for them for the entire year. Amazing! Our God is the Ultimate Provider. Since that time, three other villages have approached this man and asked him to start schools in their villages, also. Because of this man's obedience, there is now free education in four remote Himalayan villages, where the students can also learn about God's love.

Along the way, our new friend has moved closer to the villagers he and his family serve. They no longer live in a comfortable house in town, but out in the village with their three teenagers. No running water. No electricity. They don't even have the old scooter anymore.

Earlier this week, this man and his wife invited us to be the chief guests at the annual Christmas pageant at one of the schools. We jumped at the chance with a resounding, "We'd love to!" Cold rain awakened us this morning, though. For a while we debated if Steve should just go alone. Was it crazy to take the girls out in this cold rain? We finally decided to go for it, and began the process of bundling up. Eirene wore long johns under her clothes, her heaviest coat, and a hat. Isabel wore three layers of clothes below her snowsuit. Steve and I laced up our best hiking boots, buttoned our heaviest coats, packed extra clothes for the girls just in case, and asked the cook to make a load of sandwiches.

The couple picked us up in a 4-wheel drive vehicle, then drove us through 30 km of twisting, turning, bumpy, mountain roads. We could see our breath inside the jeep. Finally, we reached the town nearest the village. We parked the car and started to walk. Steve carried Eirene. I put Isabel in the baby-backpack. Then, we turned our faces into the cold rain and wind, and started the climb down to the village. Umbrellas were pointless in the strong wind. The path was slippery, but the couple insisted it would only be a 20-minute walk. One of the other village schools is a 2-hour walk from the road! Were we grateful for our warm coats and good shoes!

All of sudden, we could see it. A school for 62 students, grades K-5. What do you picture when you read the word, *school?* Here is what we saw - a low cement building, three rooms in all, each about 15 feet square, each with a door to the outside. No electricity. No heat. Just a cement building in the middle of nowhere, filled with the most adorable children you've ever seen.

They all stood as we entered, and greeted us with "Good morning, Madam," and "Good morning, Sir" in unison. They placed garlands of marigolds around our necks and instructed us to sit on the only bench. The children all sat on the floor. One of the teachers said he was guessing it would snow later in the day. I looked around and realized that almost every child had bare feet. Those who did have socks needed new ones. Never again will I complain of cold feet when mine are encased in waterproof, leather hiking boots! Later, we learned that the children had removed their shoes before entering the classroom, but still, when they went to put on their shoes, most were only flip-flops.

So, there we were, the rich Americans, sitting in the place of honor, garlands around our necks, blond-haired babies on our knees, and the pageant began. Since I have participated in and watched Christmas pageants every year of my life, I thought I'd seen everything. Shepherds wear their father's bathrobes. Angel choirs have tinsel halos. I'm telling you right now, you haven't seen the story of the birth of Jesus until you've seen it in India. Mary was all dressed up in her mother's blue sari. Herod was attended by kowtowing servants, and those Wise Men knew how to give him the homage due a king. They salaamed and bowed like no American child would ever know how to do. The angel flew around and yelled at the shepherds to not be afraid.

Shyness? Nowhere. The children spoke their lines with relish and volume. Then came the dancing. One of the boys played the Indian drum like a professional while the girls performed the local mountain dances. Singing finished it off. First, they sang translations of western Christmas carols, then their own, local songs about the birth of Jesus. Through it all, we felt their shy glances to make sure we were paying attention. Eirene clapped along with the songs, and Isabel even sang out once in a while with her baby squeaks. I don't remember when we've had a better day.

As the lone Westerners and special guests, we were expected to say something. The children waited patiently while we yammered for a few minutes, and finally came the fun - presents! They asked Eirene to hand the presents to each child. What she would have missed if Steve had come alone. We were close to the end of the gift distribution when we noticed that after each child opened his/her gift, not a single one ate any of the goodies.

"Amazing," we said to each other. "If these were kids from back home, they would have already eaten all their candy." These children, though, for whom candy is a once-in-a-year treat, were waiting to take their candy home and share it with their families.

Pretty soon it was over. We drank some warm chai (tea), ate some cookies, and then it was time to walk back up to the road. What had taken 20 minutes to walk down, took an hour to walk up. Yes, it was still raining. Yes, it was freezing cold. We didn't complain this time, though. We were too full to complain. We marveled at the fresh, new perspective of the too-well-known Story. We were grateful to have spent a whole day with our new friends and the children. We were humbled as we remembered the big, warm living room waiting for us at the end of the ride. The children we'd just met live in homes very like the school: all cement, no heat.

So grateful to God for opening our eyes to more of His world,
Robin, for us all

28 January 2002
Dear Friends and Family,

My parents came to visit us for Christmas! Yay! They arrived on the 22nd. We met them at the airport. Not as easy as it might sound. We left here on a Tuesday afternoon. The drive down the mountain to the train station took an hour. The train ride to Delhi took seven hours. The drive to the hotel took about 30 minutes. How far did we travel? 284 km (190 miles). Yes. It took us over eight hours to travel 190 miles. Back home, it takes less than half that amount of time. I will never again take such efficiency for granted.

We spent a wonderful few days in Delhi. Nice to have a little family vacation. Isabel even had her first McDonald's french fry. You have never eaten at McDonalds until you've tried their Indian potato patty burger or chicken burger with green sauce! No beef products sold here.

We debated the best way to return home. Should we all come back on the train, or would it be easier to hire a taxi? Lugging 70-pound suitcases through the New Delhi railway station didn't sound pleasant. After much thought and debate, hiring a taxi seemed the way to go. Knowing what I know now, we should have opted for the train.

First, there was the issue of finding a taxi in the first place. One year ago, the Delhi government decreed that all taxis and auto-rickshaws must run on natural gas. No more diesel or petrol powered vehicles allowed. Taking diesel and gasoline powered taxis and autos off the streets would help reduce the dangerously high air pollution levels. Not a bad idea, except that no one thought to build new natural gas stations. Here we are, one year later and there still aren't enough natural gas stations around town. Taxi and auto-rickshaw drivers line up all night long at the few stations that exist in order to fill up their tanks. The poor drivers sleep in their cars, waiting in lines that stretch for blocks. So, the first question was, could we even find a taxi to hire?

Second question - if we found a taxi, would it be able to take us home? Delhi, like Washington D.C., is a federal district. Since only taxis within the city must use clean gas, there truly are no natural gas stations outside of Delhi.

In the end, we hired a private vehicle. One way taxi companies circumvent the law is by setting aside certain vehicles from their fleets as *private*, thus making them immune to the clean gas law. If stopped by police, passengers are instructed to say that their dear friends offered the use of their car. Thankfully, no one stopped us on the way. There's no way we could have pulled off whatever conversation that would have required. God was kind to us newbies.

Remember that 8-hour trip to Delhi? It took 10 hours to get home. Ten. To drive 190 miles.

First, there are no actual highways. No long, flat stretches of road with grassy medians, exit ramps and fast cars. Here, the highway is everybody's way. Towns and villages line almost every stretch of the road. Pedestrians and bicycles fight for space along the edges.

Motorcycles swerve around both. Cows roam freely. There are no lanes. Ox carts piled high with sugar cane plod down the middle of the road forcing traffic on both sides to slow down. Busses zoom past, missing everyone by inches. In the middle of all the chaos, cars try to maneuver. On the best of days, travel in India is slow. (Sidenote: some of you have asked if we're nervous about the current tension between India and Pakistan. In a word, no. Now that you have a glimpse of how difficult it is to travel in this country, you have a better idea of why. On the map, Pakistan looks close, but when it takes 10 hours to travel less than 200 miles, close is relative.)

The second reason it took so long to get home was because our car was the fleet owner's personal vehicle. He must have made the driver swear on his life that he wouldn't damage the car. There we were in this huge SUV, one of the biggest vehicles on the road, and yet our driver never shifted higher than third gear. Unbelievable.

Sorry to complain. We had a marvelous visit with my folks. All too soon it was time to take them back to Delhi (this time, by train), and then they were gone. We're so grateful that they came, but it was hard to see them go.

The new interns arrived today. Please pray that we'll have insight and discernment to mentor them well in engineering and spiritual matters. We look forward to what God has in store for this new year. He has such great things in store for all of us.

Happy New Year!
The Smiths4

15 February 2002

Dear Mom and Dad,

It's not quite 8 am. I'm here in our living room sitting by the buchari, typing to you. Feels like you're sitting right here next to me. Did I tell you that we switched bucharis? The one that we used during your visit was made of such thin metal that the heat finally caused the door to warp. Smoke just poured out of the gaps. So frustrating. The house maintenance man told us there was an extra buchari down in the storage room. Why not give it a try? He and Steve moved out the bad one, carried up the "new" one, got the pipe up the chimney, lit a fire, and poof, smoke came pouring out of the door. How familiar! Now we know why it was in storage.

In other news, Steve and I discovered that the house help hadn't received a raise in two years. After getting advice from local

Indian friends, we raised their salary by 15%. Informed them yesterday. We also decided to hire a new cook. We know him from church. A really nice guy. There's already a different atmosphere in the kitchen with the former cook gone. Soon after we fired him, he showed up to tell us he'd been hired at the local boarding school. We were thrilled for him, then discovered later that it was a lie. Not only does he not have a new job, no one even knows he was fired. Apparently, he's claiming to be on holiday. Such denial and deception. It's good he's gone. We still pray for him and want the best for him, but he doesn't know he has a problem.

I spoke with Steve last night. He's enjoying the project trip in the mountains, but said he's never felt such cold. Though temperatures reach about 40F during the day, the warmth doesn't penetrate the house where they're staying. The pipes will remain frozen until spring, so they have a bucket of water in their room for toilet flushing and face washing. Unfortunately, the water in the bucket grows a layer of ice on it each night while they sleep, even though they light a small buchari in their room each night. Steve sleeps in all his clothes, which keeps him warm, but all the blankets and clothing keep him from rolling over in his sleep. Poor guy actually has to wake up to roll over.

Love from all of us buchari lovers,
Robin, for us all

28 February 2002
Dear Mom and Dad,

Steve just got back from his trip. Here are some of his thoughts:

> I was praying that God would reveal Himself during the project trip, that instead of concentrating only on our skills and work, we would see Him working in significant ways. This is a common prayer of mine these days. It's the opposite of my typical prayer - "Lord, help me do such and such, or Help me to be such and such." Instead, these days, I hear myself say, "God, I want to see You at work. Come down and work in a way that is undeniably You. I want to see Your hand move upon people and accomplish things that I cannot." This is just a small glimpse of what we're learning here on the other side of the world. All we can say is, "More, Lord!"

Also, Isabel had another urinary tract infection. Yesterday, she had a fever of 104.5 F but no other symptoms, just like when she was 2-months old. Our wonderful missionary doctors took good care of her. She's to take oral meds for 10 days, then wait for two, and then go back for another urine sample to make sure all is well. This is the same regimen we followed back in Texas. Unfortunately, the doctors think it's unlikely that Isabel has had two UTIs during her first year of life without there being a physical problem. One could have been happenstance. Two, though, probably not. Please don't worry. You saw how good our doctors are. Just please pray for Isabel's healing. If she does, in fact, have an anatomical problem, one solution is daily medicine for years. Sigh. The doctors said that girls usually outgrow these issues by the age of five, which is good news, of a sort. Just pray.

Love,
Robin, for us all

15 March 2002
Dear Mom and Dad,

In January, clouds settled low on our town, snow began to fall, and that was it. No sunshine from then until today. We were pretty miserable. Can laugh about it now (the sun is shining!), but two weeks ago, we weren't laughing. Sleet fell for two days. The power kept going

out. Then, the town's main water pump broke which meant no water for anyone. After five days, we decided we just had to bathe. Steve put two pots on the stove and began filling them with snow. Know how much snow it takes to fill two pots with water? Finally, there was enough for a bucket bath, which is exactly what it sounds like. You squat down next to a bucket of water, dump a scoop of water over your head, soap up, and then dump more water over your head to get the soap off. It's effective, but freezing, no matter how hot that water is.

Thankfully, the power was on that night. The space heater was blowing at full power. Steve carried the pots of warm water into the bathroom, set them down on the floor, and then, the lights went out. Of course. Why was I surprised? The bathroom went pitch black. I could see nothing. All candles and flashlights were in the bedroom on the other side of that door. Thing was, I couldn't make myself actually open the door. All that lovely, warm air would be sucked right out into that freezing cold hallway. And some people think that bathing by candlelight is romantic.

Now, here it is, two short weeks later. The sun is shining. Sky is bright blue. The mountains are glorious with their snow-capped peaks, and I wouldn't want to be anywhere else. It is my privilege, Mom and Dad, to share our lives with you by email. We will never be the same.

Love,
Robin, for us all

30 March 2002
Dear Mom and Dad,

Much of life here is starting to become routine, but some aspects still shock us, such as how often we go to the hospital. The janitors greet us like old friends when we arrive, while Eirene makes a beeline for her favorite nurses. Pneumonia, Giardia, dysentery, typhoid. We've had it all, and it's changed us. We now freely discuss tummy woes at the dinner table. Apparently we're not the only ones who discuss these issues freely. When we met our neighbours' houseguests recently, the husband said, "Oh, Steve and Robin! We missed meeting you at the worship service yesterday. Heard you had diarrhea really bad, Steve. How are you feeling?"

The latest trip to the hospital was after I missed a step walking down some stairs, tore ligaments in my left ankle, and needed a cast. Unfortunately, the physician's assistant who set the cast didn't do a very good job. Now, if I sit too long, my foot goes numb for lack of blood flow. Just stand up and walk round, right? Get that circulation going again, right? Except today horseflies decided that my toes which poke out of the end of the cast looked good to eat. I didn't feel a single bite. By the time I finally noticed and shooed them away, it was too late. My toes were swollen and bumpy. Like, *toad* bumpy. The janitors were happy to see us again when we stopped by the hospital for this latest round of antibiotics.

Please don't think that I'm looking for pity by sharing these stories. Or sainthood. Believe me, my attitude is less-than-saintly about these issues most days. I share only for one reason - to let you know that in the midst of the struggles, we're learning truths about God. Take Psalm 23. Most of us have it memorized. We know it so well that we skip over it when reading our Bibles. Here's the thing - it's true! God really is the Good Shepherd. Like David, we, too, can live free from the fear of evil.

The fear of evil. In Hebrew, *fear* is *yare*. It means the obvious (to be afraid of someone or something), but also to stand in awe of or greatly admire someone who possesses great power. Hence, we're told repeatedly in Scripture to fear (yare) God, but not evil. So, what is *evil?* There's the obvious definition (something wicked), but sometimes the word is used to mean simply less than perfect. In Genesis at one point, malnourished cows are described as being evil in appearance.

Where I am going with this? Through these unexpected troubles, I (we) are learning what it means to be in awe of God instead of evil, no matter if it's something truly wicked or merely an inconvenience or frustration. We want to hold God in high esteem, not the bad things happening to us or around us. We want to put our energy and effort into paying attention to Him instead of evil. The choice is ours - be in awe of and consumed by God, or be awed by evil. We're learning to choose God.

Love,
Robin, for us all

29 April 2002
Dear Mom and Dad,

There were huge storms last week - torrential rain, wind, thunder and lightning, even hail. Of course, as soon as the thunder began, the city turned off the power, so we were without electricity for two days. The municipality doesn't want the system damaged by the storms, so they turn things off when the weather gets bad (I guess that's one approach.) After the storms passed, we realized that somewhere along the way the phone lines had also gone down. That was four days ago. Hopefully, the phones will be fixed by tomorrow, but since I can hear the beginnings of a new storm outside right now, I won't hold my breath.

Last Wednesday, we woke to clouds, cold wind and lightning, and then we got nervous. It was supposed to be Isabel's first birthday party that day. Yikes! Thing was, we couldn't have a party without inviting the interns, the house helpers and their families, so there were 23 people signed up to attend this thing before we even issued an invitation! In the end, 43 people (including three babies Isabel's age) helped us celebrate Isa's first birthday. All seemed blessed, too, to hear the story of her name. I was so glad for the chance to tell the house help that her name means *consecrated to God.*

We've learned over the past months that names and their meanings are very important here. During a recent worship service, we learned that the pastor was asked to name a set of twins. After the parents asked him, he prayed all week, and then during the Sunday service, he named those 2-week-old babies. Yet another addition to the list of Things We've Never Seen Before.

Looks like it's going to be a busy summer. Eight new interns are coming. We don't have room for everyone here, so some will stay in a nearby guest house. Also, three new projects will start this summer though four are still ongoing. What's Hebrew for *busy*, I wonder?

We're feeling pretty stretched by living here in this house, constantly surrounded by others. Personalities within the house sometimes rub. Can someone say, *character building*? Pray that we'll have wisdom to draw the appropriate boundaries around our family of four.

We love you both, so much,
Robin and all

13 May 2002
Dear Mom and Dad,

For the past month, I thought I had a virus, but it turned out to be Giardia. Again. One of our wonderful doctors prescribed the right stuff, so I'm getting better, but when I woke up yesterday (Mother's Day), Steve was sicker than I'd seen him in a long time. Looked like a bus had run over him. Unfortunately, we were on duty for Sunday School that day, so the girls and I walked down to church while he stayed in bed. One of the interns carried Isabel while another one carried the backpack with the Sunday School supplies. Meanwhile, Eirene walked most of it on her own (45 minutes). She took a few piggy back rests on me, but not long ones. She's so fit! Amazing the difference a few months can make. After the service, the interns went out to eat, so we girls were on our own. Most of the road is closed for repairs, but I hired a taxi to take us as far up the hill as it could. He dropped us right where the road is steepest, but beggars can't be choosers, right? I carried Isabel on my back, but Eirene walked the whole way up. Story telling to the rescue! Cinderella and the prince had just begun to live happily ever after when we reached our gate. Saw that Steve was still sleeping, so I made grilled cheese sandwiches with the only bread in the house - cinnamon. Quite the Mother's Day brunch.

About mid-afternoon, Steve started to shake. Violently. If he'd been holding a glass, the water would've spilled out. I called the doctor. Should I bring Steve in, or wait until Monday morning? I described his symptoms: Shaking. Sweating from both fever and cold. A little diarrhea, but not much. Weakness. Nausea. The doctor said to bring him in right away, and to also pack a bag because he was probably going to spend the night. We needed a blood sample, fast.

I hung up the phone, packed the backpack, asked one intern to watch the girls, then instructed another to drive Steve on the scooter as far as the road would allow. I hiked the trail and met them there, then helped poor Steve walk the rest of the way to the hospital.

The doctor was delivering a baby when we arrived. Incredible to sit there and hear only silence....then that newborn wail. Beautiful! When the doctor finally came to us in the ICU, he said the symptoms sounded like dengue fever, but he'd have to run blood tests, and that Steve would definitely stay the night. Dengue? All day, I'd been consumed by self-pitying thoughts like *can't Steve just try harder on my day?* and *who makes grilled cheese for herself on Mother's Day?* Meanwhile, Steve might have dengue? Oh Lord, forgive my selfish heart!

Steve decided against a private room. Said that being with people took his mind off the pain. Doctor understood. They hooked up an IV, we ordered dinner from the kitchen, then sat to wait for the test results. Some of the interns visited, which was nice, but then it started getting dark and Steve wanted me home to put the girls to bed. Test results still weren't back, but Steve was right. I needed to go. He was in good hands, so I went home, put the girls to bed, called you and Steve's mom for Mother's Day, then fell asleep full of regret. It's now Monday. As soon as I finish this email, Eirene and I will go visit him.

We're tired, Mom. Tired of illness. Tired of living in a place with so much disease. Why do we have to live here? Why couldn't we live somewhere easier or cleaner or nicer or less stressful?

Self-pity. Not nearly as satisfying as one would hope.

In other news, Isabel's birthday package actually arrived! The girls love the books. Eirene often borrows them from her sister, but never sleeps with them. She sweetly insists I give them right back to Isabel. And yes, you read right. Eirene sleeps with books. Her favourites get tucked into bed right next to her!

Love you,
Robin

15 May 2002
Dear Mom and Dad,
Here's a final update on Steve:
Eirene and I went directly to the ICU on Monday, but it was

empty. Where was Steve? Seems that after I left the night before, things got really busy, so the doctor moved him to a semi-private room down the hall. It had beds for five people and one attached bathroom.

The ceiling was a maze of empty pipes, each one hanging horizontally from the ceiling. At one time, privacy sheets must have hung from the pipes (think curtain rods) to afford the patients some level of privacy, but now they are just old, rusty pipes. Steve reported that after he'd moved in, the diarrhea had started, so he spent the night taking trips from bed to bathroom. Problem was, he was connected to his IV which hangs on a tall, wooden stand with no wheels, and Steve's bed was about four feet off the floor. To get to the bathroom, he had to crawl down out of bed, pick up the wooden stand, walk a couple of feet, stop to tilt the stand down to get it under the pipe suspended from the ceiling, take a few steps, and then stop again to get under the next pipe...and all so the guys with diarrhea could find relief in the bathroom on the other side of the room where he had to be sure to not slip on the wet, tile floor. Later, the whole thing in reverse to get back to bed. Crazy. But then, it gave him a chance to meet his roommates. Tibetans. A couple even spoke English. One began carrying the stand for Steve on his many trips across the room. Turns out, he is also a Christian. He and Steve spent the night sharing their testimonies with each other so that, though he was obviously tired when we saw him, he was also in good spirits.

I left Eirene with her dad, then went to find the doctor. Guess what? Steve doesn't have dengue! Isn't that GREAT?! The doctor was convinced of dengue at first, but when the diarrhea finally set in (about 18 hours after the other symptoms), he took a stool sample. Steve has dysentery. The doctor confided that he hadn't seen that much blood in a stool sample for a long time, but we're relieved it isn't dengue. He had to spend all Monday attached to the IV, but then was allowed to come home that night. Returned twice on Tuesday for more fluids.
Poor Steve. It was his birthday! What a way to celebrate.

Eirene and I made two cakes: a blueberry one using the dried blueberries you brought at Christmas, and a pudding cake. We baked all morning and served them after lunch, but he didn't feel good enough to eat much. Just little bites of each. I felt so bad for him.

Thankfully, he's doing much better now. Getting his strength back slowly, but the aftereffects of dysentery are nothing compared to dengue, especially considering that he has to lead a project trip down in the plains next week. Daily temps down there hover over and above 120F these days (really!). Thank you for your prayers. We felt covered and protected and, mostly, loved.

I'm feeling weary. Dealing with Steve's illness, and now with new interns who arrived last night and are asking the same old questions (Why do Indians do _____ this way? How do I take a shower?) has just drained me. To be honest, I can't imagine living here for a whole other year, much less any time after that.

It's stressful being surrounded by people constantly, and always having something to fix. This 150+ year old house needs constant repair. The Indian-made car always needs tweaking. The other night, things came to a head. I told Steve my feelings. Said that he's often so consumed with work that I feel pushed aside, forgotten. Took me a while to admit that, though. He asked me what was wrong. Instead of answering, get this (how self-centered can I be?), I said I didn't want to tell him. I knew that if I did, he'd apologize and I'd have to forgive him, and I wasn't ready to do that. I wanted to be angry at him. What is wrong with me? Oh, but, Steve is amazing! He said I didn't have to forgive him if I wasn't ready. He understood and loved me as I was. It was exactly what I needed to hear. It gets better (or worse) though. He still had the IV shunt in his arm and was dealing with the after-affects of dysentery, but here was his hysterical wife telling him he doesn't pay her enough attention. Oh God, forgive me.

We're doing better today, but I want to get out of here. I've had enough of the interns' questions. Am just worn out.

I was in reading Nehemiah this morning about how he moved to Judah. He saw a need, felt the call to go, God gave him favor with the king, and he left. The people of Judah needed him, too. He was the guy for the time. I was impressed with the feeling this morning that our situation is similar. We, too, are far from home. We, too, saw a need, heard a call, and experienced God's favor on the plan. God knows how tired I am. If I let Him console me and give me strength, it'll be OK.

Now you know how I'm doing - bone weary, but trying to let the Lord heal and comfort me instead of comforting myself by escaping to the TV or a book. We covet your prayers.

Love,
Robin, for us all

20 May 2002
Dear Mom and Dad,

Thank you for your note. I wish I could explain with words how incredibly wonderful it is to hear that you've been praying. I easily forget to pray. How is that? I'm the one living through this stuff, but I'm the one who doesn't pray? It's so wonderful that our Lord doesn't condemn me, but instead puts me/us on the hearts of people like you who are faithful to pray. Thank you. We couldn't survive here without your prayers.

God is good! Have I said that, yet? He's so very good. Most days, in the middle of all my busyness, I look around in astonishment and wonder, and ask Him in my heart, *Lord, how is it that You've seen fit to allow us to live in this wonderful place, involved in these wonderful things?* It's so amazing to me.

Do you remember how, years ago, I applied to teach in several boarding schools around the world? Nothing ever came together, and I couldn't figure it out. Eventually married Steve, but then going overseas became fuzzier than ever. Being here, doing what we're doing, this is right. I know it, though I have no idea for how long. If, in two years, God says, "that's all for now," well, we'll come home, but for now, no matter how weary I feel at times, this is exactly what we're supposed to be doing.

I have never been so busy in my life. For the house help, I am memsahib. For the interns, I'm a mentor. For the girls, I'm mom. Wife to Steve. Daughter of God. I crawl into bed tired each night, but when I'm in the kitchen, doing the memsahib thing, I love it. When I'm one-on-one with an intern, I love it. Whether I'm doing a little school work with Eirene or playing with Isabel, I just love it. I also love the quiet morning hours when it's just the Lord and I, and yes, when I'm alone with Steve, I love that, too!

Life here isn't easy. The illnesses. The cold. Running out of water. Confusion. Frustration. Living here is harder than I imagined it would be. I also feel more at home here than I ever thought I could.

Steve's on a project trip down in the plains this week. He sounded good on the phone last night, though it's hot down there and he's still weak from last week's illness. At some point this week, they were riding an overnight train. At 3:00 in the morning, it was 98F inside the train. It averages 115F in the city where they're working. This ain't no mere Texas heat! Please continue praying for Steve. While you're at it, pray for us girls, too. Isabel woke up this morning with diarrhea all over her bed. I took a stool sample down to the hospital. While waiting to hear the test results, I discovered that Eirene has a fever of 102.1. But, God is good. The girls are sleeping, the cooks are making dinner, and I'm not down in the heat of the plains. Yes, I'm sick of being sick. Many days, I want to beg the enemy to leave us alone. In saner moments, I remember that the King is actually able to fight these battles, and so I pray. Why do I so often forget to pray?...which gets me back to where I started this letter.

I miss you.
Love,
Robin, for us all

27 May 2002

Good morning, Mom and Dad!

Just when I thought life couldn't get any weirder.

The main road is still closed for construction, so we're still walking to church and back on Sundays. On the trek home last week, it was hot, we were tired, and the hill was steep. At some point, I noticed a bug hovering around my left eye. I tried to wave it off, but next thing I knew, it was in my eye. Not like that's never happened before. It's a nuisance, but whatever. I stopped walking, declared the obvious, "There's a bug in my eye," then swiped at my eye with my fingers. Still felt the bug, so I did that thing with my eye lid where you lift the top lid over the bottom one. Did it again. And again. Finally said, "Well, I guess it's out," and we resumed our walk.

When we got home, my eye was still irritated. An hour later, it still bothered me. I kept fiddling with my eye so much that Steve finally shined a flashlight on it to see if he could see anything. I tried flushing it with water, then with saline solution. Nothing worked. Then, it got worse. Five hours later, I couldn't open my eye. It was all puffy and watery. People in the house were asking if I was on drugs.

Steve finally called the doctor. "Hi. Steve here." (Yes, we call so often that no last name is necessary.) The doctor had me do a little eye test over the phone, which apparently I failed because he said we'd better come down to the hospital. Unbelievable. For a bug in my eye?

Our poor doctor. When we arrived at the hospital, we found him in ICU with all five beds full. One patient had a heart attack while we stood right there. And I had a bug in my eye? The doctor found a heavy-duty light. You remember in MASH when Hawkeye would do surgery and with a huge lamp shining down on the patient? That's what this was. The doctor looked all over my eye with this huge lamp/spotlight thing. Couldn't find a thing. I started wondering if stress had finally sent me over the edge. Finally, the doctor wondered aloud if the bug had scratched the white part of my eye, kind of like a cat on a blackboard. The burning and itching were probably due to a scratch, so I should wear a patch on my eye for the night, also put some cream on it, and I'd probably feel better tomorrow.

So, we arrived back at home, me with a patch covering the left side of my face, all because of some dumb, kamikaze bug. Unbelievable. Went to bed. And so began the weirdest night of my life. I would doze for a while, but then be awakened by a burning, itching sensation in my eye. Finally, I decided I really must be going crazy now because the pain seemed to move around. What in the world? I tore the bandage off about 2 am, and started rubbing my eye like a madman. If I could have taken out my eye and rinsed it off, I would have.

The next morning, all I could do was lie in bed. I was exhausted, sure, the patch made me feel weird, too. I lost all sense of depth perception, and looking at people out of my good eye, while trying to keep the other one closed under the patch was hard so that I finally just lay down and closed my eyes. Steve called the doctor about noon to say that the pain hadn't subsided. Doctor said we should see an eye specialist. No way.

After lunch, we ordered a taxi to meet us at the bottom of the hill, and by 3:00 that afternoon, there we were, driving the one-hour drive down the mountain to the state capital. All for a bug in my eye? Took us some running around to find the doctor, but we finally found the right place. He had all the fancy, latest equipment. I put my chin on the little shelf of one of his machines, he looked through his big microscope at my eye, then loudly proclaimed, "You've got baby bugs in there!"

Yes, there were larvae in my eye. Crawling larvae. In my eye. Fifteen. I counted as he removed them. 15! Larvae! IN MY EYE!

Turns out, the burning sensation during the night which felt like it was moving around REALLY WAS MOVING AROUND IN MY EYE! There were live baby bugs in my eye. Completely, totally, exhaustibly unbelievable.

The specialist was thorough. And kind. Once he was satisfied they were all out, he gave me some drops, directed me to use them every hour for two days, and then we were done. Got home and completely grossed out the interns with the story. The new ones who arrived last week aren't sure what to think about this country. One of them has already been in the hospital for three days with dysentery, then I had this eye thing, and now the country's almost at war with Pakistan. ????

Last night, once the anesthesia wore off, I felt like someone actually had taken my eye out, washed it, and put it back in. I went to bed about 8:30. Steve didn't stay up too much later. Sheer exhaustion for both of us. Of course, I woke up before 4:00 am (which is why I have access to a computer and am writing you), but that's OK because for the first time in 48 hours, my eye isn't patched, nothing burns, nothing is CRAWLING around inside it, I have depth perception, and I'm laughing. Been laughing a lot. It started when I heard we had to go to the hospital on Sunday. I laughed when I put on the patch. I was laughing on the back of the scooter as we rode home and it started to downpour, a deluge, right after the doctor said to make sure to keep the patch nice and dry! I was laughing as I walked in the door, soaking wet, mascara streaming out of my one good eye, patch over the other, and Eirene said, "Mama, you look awful!" I don't think I'm crazy, though. Not yet. I wasn't laughing when I couldn't sleep. I wasn't laughing when we couldn't find the doctor in the city, and I wasn't laughing when he was picking nits out of my eye. I did laugh, though, when he let Steve look through the microscope for the fun of it, and Steve declared, "That's disgusting!"

Must admit, I'm half afraid I might never want to go outside again. The doctor said that the eggs were probably dangling from the insect's abdomen, and that she dropped them as soon as she touched my eye. He then admitted that this kind of thing could have happened anywhere. Eggs could have dropped out of a tree! Can you imagine? I'm thinking it's time to develop the world's first pair of walking safety goggles?

I sure love you guys. Thanks for listening, and when you're done laughing, please do pray for us. One of the long term staff in the house shook his head at my story and said, "Robin, why do these things keep happening to you?" I said I didn't know, that if God is trying to get our attention, apparently we're missing it, but if the enemy is against us, apparently our prayers aren't working. I told him to pray and ask the Lord, and to let me know if he hears anything. He said, "Robin, we sure appreciate you." I think I needed to hear that. And I'll tell you the same thing I said to him, "Let us know if God tells you anything."

These things are funny, but Steve is feeling overwhelmed and vulnerable. He cried last night. He's just so tired of somebody always being sick in our family. He can't protect any of us here. In the last 3 weeks alone, Isabel's been sick twice, Eirene once, Steve & I one each, and now bug babies. How do you protect your wife from bug larvae?

Love, from your safety goggle-wearing daughter,
Robin

In the spring of 2002, rumors of war began to circulate around our town. Dormant angers concerning the Indian state of Kashmir had been awakened.

When India and Pakistan became independent nations in 1947, the prince of Kashmir dreamt of ruling a sovereign kingdom, a thoroughly unrealistic idea. Both the new Pakistan and the new India wanted to rule the area. Sure enough, soon after independence was declared, the new Pakistan sent troops into Kashmir. The prince appealed to new India for help, but the governor-general demanded that he accede his kingdom to India first. Left with no choice, the prince declared his allegiance to India. Indian troops crossed the border and drove the Pakistani soldiers from all but one section of the new Indian state. That "Line of Control" between India and Pakistan has been tense ever since. Twice, the two nations went to war over the area, first in 1965 and again in 1999.

In December 2001, while we were preparing to spend our first Christmas in India, five armed men attacked the parliament building in Delhi. They killed seven people before being killed by Indian soldiers. India blamed Pakistan, and then deployed increased troops to the border. Soon, both sides moved ballistic missiles close to the border. In January, both sides reported receiving artillery fire from the other side. More troops were mobilized. Violent clashes resulted in deaths on both sides. In May 2002, the Prime Minister expelled the Pakistani High Commissioner from the country, and then ordered his troops to prepare for a decisive battle. Neither side recused the option of using their nuclear weapons. Most world leaders believed war was inevitable. The many embassies located in Delhi, including the American embassy, quickly emptied as everyone but essential staff was sent home. Mission agencies recalled their people. NGOs closed their doors. The world watched and waited.

Thankfully, eventually, tensions eased. Troops on both sides slowly demobilized until, in November 2003, a cease-fire was signed. Actual war had been avoided, but casualties were high on both sides. I'm getting a bit ahead of our story, though. Let's go back to June 2002. Up in the mountains, we felt far removed from these events, but family back in the States were understandably concerned. The following emails were written during the most tense time, after the Prime Minister told his troops to prepare for that decisive battle.

5 June 2002

Dear Mom and Dad,

It was so good to talk to you earlier this week. I'm sorry that so many people are concerned for our safety. We are fine. We are safe and, honestly, feel isolated from what you see on the news. From our perspective, it seems like there's just some sword rattling going on between Pakistan and India, not to say that Steve and I are ignoring events. We are in regular contact with the embassy, and, like you, are watching the news.

I'll write more in a couple of days. For now, please enjoy the note below. I wrote it last month, but couldn't send due to travels. May it be a lighthearted touch in the midst of this current conflict.

About 9:30 the other evening, Steve and I realized that we'd just survived our busiest day ever. Issues started at 7:00 that morning, and we were still going 9:30 that night. We were so exhausted that we made a list of everything we'd done, and I was determined to tell you about each and every detail. I tried to convince myself that I wanted to tell you about everything to give you a glimpse of a "day in the life." In reality, I was looking for pity.

What I can share is the important lessons we're learning these days:

- It's OK to shut the door.
- Training our girls is more important than mentoring the interns.
- It's very easy to shift from being a married couple to mere roommates.

We're also learning that we're surrounded by people whose lives are so much harder than ours. One of our cooks was married when he was 13. Years ago, his parents tricked him into coming home from his schooling in Delhi, and married him to a local girl. How's that for a welcome home party? He's now in his late twenties. His parents are pressuring him to come get his "wife" from the village. Our cook became a Christian when he was in high school. The lady is Hindu. What should he do? Is he technically married, even though child marriages are against official law? Illiterate villagers don't know or care about law books. In their eyes, she is his wife. How does he stand against his whole family with love and humility?

Every Thursday evening we host a small group from church in our home. Two ladies faithfully attend each week. Both are single moms. Their husbands deserted them, though we're told repeatedly, "there is no such thing as divorce in this country." I understand that being a single mom is difficult everywhere, but being a single mom here, where there is no Coats for Kids, welfare, soup kitchens or Salvation Army thrift stores is especially difficult. One of the husbands left years ago to live with his girlfriend. Recently, he expressed a desire to return, provided his girlfriend is allowed to come, too. Meanwhile, when the other husband left, he took two of their four children with him. The wife hasn't seen any of them since. Here's what's incredible, though - These women smile more than anyone I've ever met. During testimony time, they are the ones who talk about God's goodness.

God is watching out for these "widows." They have good jobs, both recently received raises, and not long ago, one of the women was told that someone had pledged an anonymous gift to pay for her sons' education at one of the better schools in town. God is so good.

When I think of these ladies, I can't help but ask why. Why did such things have to happen to them? It's not a unique question. People have argued why bad things happen to good people since the days of Job. Bookstore shelves are stocked with supposed answers. People lose their faith over this issue. The thing is, these ladies aren't asking why. They're too busy talking about how good God is, how He provides for them and even encourages them when they cry. While Steve and I are busy philosophizing, these ladies are just getting on with life, trusting in the One who promised to never leave them or forsake them. Each week, they share new testimonies of His goodness.

Steve and I grateful are that we get to see God at work in the lives of our friends here. Living here is the hardest thing we've ever done. Sometimes, we count the number of days we have left, but then I remember what Dad often says - life is not about us. Contrary to the self-help-talk-show-speech of modern America, life is *not* about me, but is about God and making His glory known. To that end, pray with us that He would be exalted in us, here in this town, in this country, and also right where you are.

We love you guys, so much.
Robin, for us all

8 June 2002
Hey Big Brother,

Thanks for your recent email expressing concern for us and our safety. Please know that we take none of these events lightly. We're not brushing off the news on the TV, but we have no desire to react out of fear. We are praying and asking the Lord for His direction. Our Father is rich in guidance, as you know, so we're seeking Him first before making any decisions.

To be honest, we weren't concerned about the conflict at all until we started getting phone calls from Mom and Dad who said that people were calling them with concerns.

The western and Indian perspectives of this conflict couldn't be more different. Around here, people live as if no one is threatening war at all, but where you are, people seem to think we should get ourselves to the closest air raid shelter. We're asking the Lord to give us His perspective in all this. Not the Indian. Not the Western.

I'll write to Mom and Dad as soon as I finish this letter to you. Know that we love you guys and appreciate your prayers on our behalf.

Love,
Robin, for us all

8 June 2002

Dear Mom and Dad,

The US State Department recently issued warnings to all American citizens living in India. Many embassies in Delhi, including ours, have already sent nonessential staff and family members home. World leaders seem concerned about nuclear war, but we don't think either Pakistan or India is dumb enough to actually push the button. Even so, we cannot ignore the possibility. The other main risk to us is if riots were to start. Riots would make leaving the country difficult. As of now, the streets in Delhi are quiet.

The main reason we'd leave India right now pertains to the interns. The home office recalled all of them back to the States. The last one should fly out by the end of the week. Once they're gone, the need for us to be here will diminish significantly.

I mentioned to you our plans to visit in September. Since we're now rather aimless with the interns gone, well, we decided we might as well come home now. Yay!!!! We'll return to India in early August, assuming, of course, that the current tensions don't escalate.

Meanwhile, do please join us in praying for India and Pakistan, that peace would reign, and that God would break through the significant tensions between the Hindus and Muslims.

I know you're worried. Let me reiterate: neither Steve nor I feel there is an immediate emergency situation that requires a quick evacuation. From our perspective, we're simply coming home for a longer and earlier-than-planned vacation. I'll inform you as soon as we have our flights confirmed. Until then, please know that we are keeping a close eye on the situation, and we will move up our departure date if tensions escalate.

Grace, peace, and love to you both,
Robin, for us all

12 June 2002
Dear Mom and Dad,

It's been a busy few days. We changed all the interns' flights, then escorted five down to Delhi by train yesterday. Three more will leave tomorrow, then the last will depart on Saturday. Right now, we're planning to fly out next week, and the closer it gets, the more excited we become. How we look forward to doing "normal" things like going to a movie, having a date without the girls, eating American food, drinking coffee. Eirene, meanwhile, says that she'll be very, very sad to go, and will miss her aunties (the cook and the nanny) while we're gone.

And oh, Isabel said her first word the other day! She said, "Bye-bye," complete with a queen's wave. Very cute, and also descriptive of our life here. So many people have come and gone this year that bye-bye is her first word? Nonetheless, Isabel is very proud of her accomplishment and revels in her ability to get a whole room of people waving back at her, saying bye-bye!

Looking forward to coming home to American soil,
Robin, for us all

The following is a challenging editorial that Glenn Penner, Communications Officer for *The Voice of the Martyrs*, wrote on 22 July, 2002. We read it after our return to America:

...As missionary agencies, we tend to evacuate our staff when things get "hot" in our countries of service. This became most obvious in the aftermath of the events of September 11, 2001, when many missionaries were evacuated from Pakistan and Afghanistan. Such evacuations of missionary staff are, by no means, unique.

...evacuation decisions are often taken out of the hands of the missionaries by government orders, the church's advice, or circumstances beyond their control. But...could it really be a reasonable supposition that God intends suffering for our national brethren, but not for the missionary? Would the purposes of God consistently suffer if the missionary remained in a situation of conflict?"

.....I have an appalling theology of suffering. In fact, it is hardly a theology because it cannot be supported by Scripture. For me, and I suspect for my generation, comfort and security are seen as our birthright. We strive ardently to hold on to them, hardly considering the Biblical requirement to release them for the sake of the Gospel. It's as if our motto is, 'We came to serve, not to suffer.' "

As Communications Officer for *The Voice of the Martyrs*, I receive a number of emails from all over the world...[People want to know if] it is "safe" to minister [in certain nations].

Usually, the answer is "Yes, for the most part." Usually foreigners are much safer in restricted societies than the national believers who do not have the luxury of evacuation. The worst thing that can usually happen to the foreign missionaries is that they are expelled from the country. There are rare (and tragic) exceptions, but this is generally true.

But... "Is it safe?" When is it ever safe to follow Jesus? Did Jesus promise a safe road? Is the call of God only to be followed if *to pastures green, He leadeth me?* Rather, did He not say, *If anyone would come after Me, let him deny himself and take up his cross and follow Me* (Matthew 16:24)? The path of Christ is the path of the cross. Yet, how many of us are like Peter, who upon hearing that Jesus was going to follow this path, took Him aside and began to rebuke Him, saying, ...*This shall never happen to you* (Matthew 16:22). Jesus replied, that such a mentality reflected the attitude of this world, rather than the mind of God (16:23). To the mind of God, suffering is not the worst thing that can happen to His people. Disobedience is.

17 July 2002

Dear Friends and Family,

We've been home for a month, and it's been pretty close to non-stop since we got off the plane. But, hey, we've had important things to do: movies to see, favourite stores to visit, restaurants to try. It is wonderful being home. What a joy to hug dear friends!

Our lives are marked by events. There was the year we bought our first house. The year Eirene was born. Then Isabel. This past year will go down as the Year of Sickness. Who knew that four people could need a doctor so often? Unfortunately, it's not over yet.

When Isabel was two months old, she was diagnosed with a urinary tract infection and had to stay in the hospital for three days here in Austin. The doctors ran a slew of tests, some twice, but when it was all said and done, they couldn't find an explanation for the UTI. All test results were normal. They decided, we probably wouldn't ever have to worry about it again. Must have been a fluke, and so good-bye, and have fun in India.

Seven months later, we walked home from the hospital one day (tummy issues again) to find little Isabel burning with fever. One look told us she was having another infection. We rushed back to the hospital, our doctors gave her great care, and within days she was fine. Our doctors suggested that the next time we went home to the States, we should get Isabel tested again. A second infection in less than one year was probably not coincidence. They prescribed a low-grade antibiotic, just to make sure infection didn't set in again, and we added "see doctor" to our list of things to do in America.

Two weeks ago, we took Isabel to a pediatric urologist here in Austin. He ran some tests, then came back with a diagnosis we didn't want to hear - there is scarring on her kidneys (not good), and she has low-grade reflux. It seems that when Isabel's bladder empties, some of the urine leaks from her bladder back up to her kidneys. It was his opinion that the reflux was causing the kidney infections and scarring, and that we should get surgery done right away to fix it.

We immediately went home and called our two doctors back in India and my uncle (also a doctor). All agreed that Isabel will probably need some kind of surgery, but a second opinion is important. My uncle made some calls, and then suggested we see a former colleague of his over in Houston. Two days ago, we found ourselves sitting in his office. After looking over Isabel's records and test results, he declared that he couldn't see any significant scarring on Isabel's kidneys, and with such low-grade reflux, surgical intervention wasn't necessary. Oral meds will suffice. What?!?

He suggested one more test to confirm. If test results are positive, Isabel will need surgery. That's our current situation. Hopefully, we'll have the test done some time this week. A good result means that we'll return to India in August. If she needs surgery, our return to India will be delayed.

We don't know the future, but we know God is with us. We're glad to have a plan of action, and we're surrounded by good advisors.

We're grateful for your support, and we revel in our God for Whom there is no confusion or worry. Proverbs 16:33 is true: *The lot is cast into the lap, but its every direction is from the Lord.* God does exercise control in all things. We are not in this life alone.

May His confidence be our hope,
The 4Smiths

21 July 2002
Dear Friends and Family,

Thank you for your prayers. We went to the hospital on Friday. At the last minute, the doctors suggested that Eirene also get tested, so Steve held Eirene's hand during her tests while my mom and I stayed with Isabel. Eirene's kidneys appear perfectly normal. Thank You, God!

Once Isabel's tests were done, we took all the results over to the original doctor here in Austin, the one who had recommended surgery. He compared this scan with the tests from ten days ago, and then declared everything seems fine! Apparently this second test gives a much clearer picture than the earlier ultrasound. This test shows two perfectly normal kidneys. There is no evidence of any scarring. There is no need for any surgery! Isabel does have low-grade reflux, but oral meds will suffice. What joy is in our hearts!

We're so grateful we sought a second opinion. The long day in Houston waiting to see my uncle's former colleague was more than worth it. We knew nothing about him other than Uncle Kirby said to see him. Turns out, he is the head of pediatric urology at Texas Children's Hospital in Houston, one of the best children's hospitals in the world. We probably never would have known who he is except that once all the tests were done on Friday and we went to meet with the original urologist here in Austin, he took one look at our paperwork and exclaimed, "You went to __ for a second opinion? He's the guru of pediatric urology in Texas!"

Thank you, Uncle Kirby.
Thank You, Lord!
We love you all. We'll write again once we're back in India.

Until then, grace and peace,
Robin, for us all

My dad sent the following email to the extended family after our six weeks of home-leave:

6 August 2002

Dear Family:

Robin, Steve and the Little Precious Ones have migrated back to India...Today they are on a train from Delhi [then, eventually] up the mountain by taxi to their home.

Our house is modest sized, but a big empty hole in the past few days. Mary Jo began to unravel the evidence of their 6-week stay here yesterday, most of which I will place back in the attic or in their storage unit across town.

Eirene was "using her words" very expressively, with nothing hidden. "I'm feeling kind of sad today" (mouth down-turned, eyes moist). "I'm going to miss you. Can you come to India?" Finally (in her bed with her mom and grandma on the last morning), complete tearful meltdown, mom holding her, all three of them crying.

Their life in India is rich in that there is much activity (a lot of hard work done by manual labor without all of the conveniences). Eirene has companions and a few little friends, so her days will brighten again when they reach the mountains ("It's HOT in Texas, Grandpa!"). They plan to be there for another year...

I was not prepared for the immense pull on our heart strings when one of our granddaughters used her words to express emotions of love for an entire family...The will to control mysteriously disappears, while the need to [simply] engage...takes over. I embrace and desire the...gifts that experiences [such as this] with our grandchildren deposit into our lives. We can hardly wait for more, both in India and in California [where our son and his family live].

Many people have told us how they feel about their grandchildren. Not many tell how their grandchildren make *them* feel - out of control, wonderful, sorrowful, fulfilled, meaningful, fanciful.

Love,
S and MJ

What follows are excerpts from a packing list I crafted for a new family coming to join us in India:

9 August 2002

...I wish I hadn't brought my good books. Steve and I find comfort in having our favorite books within reach, but I wish I hadn't brought them. Monsoons on this mountain are just awful. Mold is growing on our beloved books. It grows on my shoes over night. To try to keep the moisture levels down, all wardrobes have been retrofitted with light bulbs. When we have power, those lights are on. Mold on clothing is nasty! As far as food goes, we keep almost everything in plastic baggies: breakfast cereal, cookies, pasta. Even toiletries. Bring baggies, all sizes!

In summary, bring items that either (1) you won't mind leaving behind when you leave at the end of your term, or (2) you won't cry over if they get ruined. Don't bring photos if they're very special to you.

To help our family maintain some traditions, we brought our Christmas stockings and some favorite Christmas books and music. Establishing traditions with our kids is important to us, even if it ruins the items. We'll buy new, if we need to.

About clothes. Don't pack shorts. Plan to buy local, Indian dress once you arrive. Just remember, whatever you bring will probably get ruined. It's not just monsoon. Washing clothes by hand just wears them out. Life here is just harder on things. There's a reason all those home decorating books, magazines and TV shows are made in the west. None of that stuff makes sense here!

Food is complicated. This was yet another area about which Steve and I were clueless. We never realized we'd miss random goodies like blueberries or a certain type of breakfast cereal. We have coffee stashed away in our bedroom, but locally-made coffeemakers are awful. Buy a stove-top percolator at your local camping store and bring it with you if you want proper coffee in the morning.

During our home-leave, when we were packing to return, I struggled over how much luggage space to devote to food. I finally realized that, no matter how much I packed, it would eventually run out, and then what? At some point, you just have to make do with local ingredients. In the end, I decided that packing a can of something special for the Holidays was one thing, but hoarding made no sense. It's embarrassing to admit, but giving up our favorite foods has been harder than I ever would have thought. No one ever mentioned it in those so-you-want-to-be-a-missionary talks. I wish someone would have warned us. We do have maple flavoring because we can't imagine pancakes without syrup (even the homemade kind), and yes, we do have coffee, but other than that, we try to enjoy food packages when/if they come, without pining for them if they don't.

Packing for two years is overwhelming, but you can do it. The Lord will show you what to pack and what to leave behind. If you're really unsure about something, put it in a box marked "get in one year," and then put the box at the front of your storage unit. When you go home after your first year, you'll look in the box and think, *Why in the world did I ever think I'd need that in India?*

We're looking forward to your arrival.
Robin

22 August 2002
Dear Mom and Dad,

What an unexpected comfort it is to be back home! We miss you, of course, and yes, a 1/4 pound beef burger with cheddar, guacamole, grilled onions and jalapeños would taste great right now, but other than that, we've settled into our routines as if we never left. I write so often about the difficulties here. Now that we're back, we realize that life back "home" in America is hard, too.

During our visit, we shared with people about all we learned last year about life not being about us or our comfort, but being about God and making His glory (His character) known. I wish that our actions had matched our message. For every one day spent talking about how we're to live for God instead of comfort, we spent six days watching obscene amounts of television, satisfying every food craving, and staying up so late at night that we were unable to wake early enough the next day to have time with the Lord. We thought that we deserved the chance to overindulge. It was as if we'd spent months paying our dues in India, and now it was time to collect. We thought that the foods and the relaxation offered by the US culture would fill our souls. Instead, our souls got hungrier, even as our bellies grew.

We once heard an African pastor say that he and his congregation prayed for the West with all its opulence. We're beginning to understand. I'm sorry I complain about all the things we don't have here. I know now that God uses each "hardship" to push us closer to Himself, the Only One who can truly satisfy.

We're feeling a renewed sense of vision these days. Realized that at some point last year, Steve and I picked up a substitute mentality, as if we are merely stand-ins for the real family who will eventually come and run this house. After all, we only made a 2-year commitment. Now we know to reject that thought. We're not just substitutes. We are not just biding our time here while waiting for a chance to return permanently to the US.

What does God have for us after this year? We're trusting Him to make His will clear, and we will go wherever He takes us. We're more certain than ever that He is in charge, He is adamant in His love for and pursuit of us, and His will is the greatest thing we can embrace for ourselves, our girls, and for His Kingdom.

Love you both,
Robin and all

25 August 2002
Dear Mom and Dad,

In a recent email, a friend told me that the root word for *vacation* means to make empty (think vacate or vacant*)*. However, the human soul can't become vacant. Even when we clear our calendars, our minds fill up with something. Therefore, the Hebrew idea of *holiday*, a holy day that is time set apart for the Lord, is a better concept. Jesus often *drew away to a lonely place to rest* after a time of intense ministry.

Her point resonated with me. I had never thought to compare the concept of holiday with vacation. How good of God, the Good Father, to give the Israelites holy days for their days off, not just vacation time. Now that I think about it, I have a chance for a holiday every week, don't I? It's called Sunday. How often do I set aside that day as holy? Usually, Sunday is the busiest day of my week! Gives me a lot to think about.

Love,
Robin, for us all

21 September 2002
Dear Mom and Dad,

Steve here, writing to let you know that Robin and I are not doing well these days. We feel distant from each other and the Lord. A recent prayer time was so dry that I finally just stopped. Picked up a devotional book, desperate for something or someone to help channel my heart into a place of connecting with God. I read only a few sentences when the thought hit: I don't trust God.

God is refining our characters through everything we experience here. However, while reading the devotional that day, I realized that at some point last year I began to think that God is more Teacher than Father, that He'd rather teach me than love me (or us, the Smith family).

I also know now that I'm afraid of God. The trials are relentless! Within two weeks of our return, three of us were down with the flu, yet another health difficulty in this place. I was hoping and even expecting that we'd return from the US somehow more immune to the Indian viruses and bacteria. After this latest round of illness, I just finally gave in to the disappointment and hurt. I feel betrayed by God. I don't understand the need for these trials.

I understand that God wants to teach us through these trials, that He is able not only sustain us through life's pressures, but also to make us victorious. However, I can't help but question, "What kind of Father desires to put His children through pain?"

Why won't He heal us? Why doesn't He answer? My heart is hurting. I don't trust in His goodness toward me. It seems to me a loving Father would desire to heal His children. I apologize if my questions sound like blasphemy, but I think God appreciates honesty. Certainly, He is big enough to deal with my honest questions, even questions that might challenge His own character. Certainly, He is not so small as to be threatened by any question I can pose.

I shared my heart with Robin, and she agreed. She is feeling the same way, and, of course this is affecting our marriage. Before you despair for us, let me also share what God has been saying to me since that morning when I realized I don't trust Him. The next day, I was in the Word again, attempting to connect with Him. Psalm 105 talks about God delivering Israel from slavery in Egypt. I saw that His taking Israel through the Red Sea, and then through the desert, was not because He desired to challenge their character or see what they were made of. Taking His people through the Red Sea and the desert (and the trials that resulted) were actually part of Israel's very deliverance. I'm starting to see that God does not wish us pain for pain's sake, nor is He simply trying to strengthen our character. He is delivering us. Now that's something I am willing to hold onto - a loving God who wants to deliver me/make me free, not just "clean me up" at any cost.

Richard Foster wrote in *Celebration of Discipline*: *If we could make the Creator of heaven and earth instantly appear at our beck and call, we would not be in communion with the God of Abraham, Isaac, and Jacob. We do that with objects, with things, with idols. But God, the great iconoclast, is constantly smashing our false images of who He is and what He is like.*

Please don't fear for us. We are not in spiritual crisis. Life is not as bad as we sometimes project. We are in relationship with a loving, caring God. We have access to great medical help and also the Great Healer. We have friends and family who love us. Many of our neighbours here have none of those things. Yes, Robin and I are feeling a little bruised, even (dare we say it?) by God Himself. However, even in the midst of all this, we are absolutely certain that God is sufficient to carry us through this phase, to deliver us, not only from our misunderstandings about Him, but from anything that keeps us from experiencing true freedom.

We love and appreciate you.
Steve, for the family

19 November 2002
Hey Mom,

We got your package yesterday. Thank you! Steve shared the sports section with the whole office, while Eirene stuck four of the Christmas stickers to her arm and showed them off to the house help who were eating their lunch in the kitchen. Isabel saw that, of course wanted to be just like her, so I put one on her arm, too, and away she ran to the kitchen to show her aunties.

Thoughtful of you to send Thanksgiving napkins. Most of our western friends here are Brits, so they don't celebrate Thanksgiving, and since this is a Hindu nation, Christmas isn't celebrated much. All that to say, November and December are quiet around here. No crowded American malls, holiday-themed TV shows or school projects and programs.

We're still praying about what to do next year. We discuss it often, the two of us, but I wish you were here to share things with. I've been searching my heart, wondering why we'd stay or why we'd leave. God showed me one thing during Bible study time with the female interns recently. We were discussing the benefits of finding satisfaction in God. He suddenly showed me my heart. My main struggle with leaving is what will people say? If we leave, won't we be just one more short-term mission family? Living here, being missionaries, well, it gets us kudos from all over. People back home think we're doing something amazing. People here think we've adapted well, or speak the language well, or run the house well. I was dumbstruck. Had no idea that I cared that much about other people's opinions. Prayed hard over that one. Talked to Steve and discovered he was learning the same thing about himself.

In the end, we agreed that if we're going to stay, it has to be for a lot better reason than getting feedback from others. Our satisfaction must be found in God alone, not in what anyone says or thinks about us.

Love you both,
Robin, for us all

26 November 2002
URGENT PRAYER REQUESTED!

On the 17th of November, a group of 200 people attacked the house of Pastor David in the state of Maharashtra. They cut off the telephone wires, disrupted a prayer meeting, and verbally abused and threatened his wife, Jyoti, and his three children. When they found out that Pastor David was not there, they broke household items, damaged the Bible verses hanging on the walls and destroyed the church sign board. Thankfully, no one was hurt, but the mob held the family captive all day, waiting for Pastor David's return. They repeatedly warned that they had come to burn the family. When they finally left, they warned the family to leave town immediately. The house owner demanded that they vacate the house.

Pastor David's friends helped the family to move to another town. Pastor David is currently in hiding. Please pray for David and his family. He desires a permanent location for the ministry so that he can work in peace, free from the threats of a landlord.

Pastor David and his wife come from a Dalit (untouchable) background. Several years ago, a disciple of Jesus visited his village, stayed with them in their home, ate with them, and then slept on the floor of their very small hut. David's home was so small that the visitor had to raise his legs and place them on the wall while sleeping. David says that as he observed that man of God loving them, even though they are Dalits. The Gospel of love captured his heart. Today, Pastor David oversees more than 100 missionaries, and has seen more than 60 pioneer churches planted in one of the most resistant areas in the state of Maharashtra.

Thankful for your prayers,
Robin

27 November 2002
Dear Mom and Dad,

Yesterday, we had a crystal clear view of the mountains.

Breathtaking. Majestic. We're beginning to grasp the psalmist's point in Psalm 121: *I will lift up my eyes to the hills – From whence comes my help? My help comes from the LORD, Who made heaven and earth.* As we gaze out our windows on this awesome landscape, we're reminded that when life gets hard, it's easy to think about escaping into the hills. It's easy to think that "just getting away from it all" will make everything better. The psalmist discovered that "help" does not come from escape. Help comes from the One Who made the mountains: *He will not allow your foot to be moved; He who keeps you will not slumber...The LORD is your keeper, the LORD is your shade at your right hand...The LORD shall preserve your going out and your coming in from this time forth and even forevermore.*

I don't know much about rock climbing (the extreme kind), but I would imagine the worst fear is a slippery slope or unsure footing. Our Lord will not allow our feet to be moved. What a God!

Your grateful daughter,
Robin

Below is an email Steve wrote to our home church in Austin:
16 December 2002
Dear Friends,

After much deliberation, Robin and I are now settled on a decision. We love what we are doing, but at the same time, communal living and our roles here are taking a toll on us and our family. This season of our lives has been great, and we are thankful, but our life in this house will end in Aug 2003. A new staff couple who joined us two months ago have recently agreed to take over our position in August. However, we question whether it's time for us to return to Austin. God has provided teaching opportunities for us here with Indian Christians recently. One class was on finances. Not that we're experts, but even basics like budgets and savings are new concepts for these folks. Same with marriage and parenting. The upper castes have access to information because they speak English, but the working classes of India have no materials in their own language. Being able to provide them helpful tools blessed them and touched us. Now we feel stuck. Should we stay? On the other hand, do we really want to create a ministry for ourselves? Feels audacious to just hang out a sign and hope for the best.

Being exhausted doesn't help. Some days, we just want to move home, live near Robin's folks, eat hamburgers and go see a few movies. Yes, the thought of being helpful and useful to needy people is tempting, but India isn't appealing. At the same time, we know we're not the same people we were 18 months ago. Will I be fulfilled at my old engineering job? Will we feel guilty living in such an easy, comfortable place? Will we slip back into the consumerism and forget what the Lord has taught us here?

We received your email in the middle of all these questions. Your comments made us wonder if perhaps there are more options than either staying here or returning to Austin. Could it be that the Lord has something for us that's so huge and unexpected that we'd never dream it up on our own? ??? Is that even Biblical (smile)?

Robin's dad talks about "God making the phone calls." We've been praying for that, for someone to knock on our door, send us an email, or write us a letter, and then you wrote to us, asking about Turkey. Hmm....

Blessings,
Steve, with Robin

17 December 2002

Merry Christmas, Mom and Dad!

It's almost 4 am. Couldn't sleep. Finally decided to stop trying and get up. Thankfully, it's not too cold in the living room, the lingering affects of last night's buchari. Promise me you'll never take your central heating for granted!

We're well. Such a relief to not be sick at the moment. Girls are fine. Isabel was pretty cranky for a while. Pretty bad diapers. The doctor finally decided that her system is tired from all the meds she's had to take, so for two weeks she's to have absolutely no dairy or sugar to help her intestines recover. Poor thing. She likes nothing better than chai and biscuits (cookies), so for the past week we've been hearing this pitiful little, "Biscuit! Biscuit," while she points at the top of the refrigerator where we keep them.

Isabel is a goofball. She loves to laugh, and often walks around laughing aloud at nothing just to make other people laugh so that she can start laughing for real in response. She looks like me. Sometimes we wonder who in the world Eirene looks like. Speaking of whom, Eirene will be four on Sunday. Four years already? She's growing tall, like her daddy, and she loves our daily schoolwork. Isabel is much more verbal than Eirene was at that age, and is very sure of herself physically, so she's not afraid to climb to the top of the slide, or the ladder to Eirene's loft in their bedroom. Both activities, of course, scare us to death, but the girls think it's great fun.

The office administrator and his fiancé asked us to do their pre-marriage counseling. Such a privilege. He's a third generation Indian Christian; she's an American who's lived here for three years. My eyes about jumped out of my head when he asked. They seem so much more "with it" than we were when we were engaged. The wedding will be in February, Mom, right about the time you leave. We're all so excited you get to come back with us after we meet you in Thailand on our next visa run! Eirene's already talking about it.

Looking forward to seeing you soon,
Robin (and all)

19 December 2002

Merry Christmas, Family and Friends!

Tree trimmed, stockings hung, presents wrapped, lights strung. Would Christmas be Christmas without such things? Consider this scenario:

It's Christmas Day. You live with your whole family in a two-room house made of stone. The house has no heat, no bathroom. To cook, you light the one burner that's connected to the propane tank, and you cook your evening meal in your one pot. There is no extra money for presents. A piece of candy is the only gift for which your children might hope. Instead of focusing on the presents you might get this year, you celebrate the day by visiting friends and sharing your food with them. No white elephant gift exchanges, but you enjoy the conversation and the laughter.

The one decoration that you might have in your home is not a Christmas tree. Instead, hung up high for all to see, maybe even outside by your front door, is a paper star. Red or gold, decorated or plain, the star is there to announce the Day. Why a star? The answer is found in the *Vedas*, the oldest of all Hindu scriptures. It is a well-known prayer - *From the unreal lead me to the real; from darkness lead me to light; from death lead me to immortality.*

Scripture tells us that Christ's birth was announced to sages in the East through His star. Like the Israelites, the people of the East were also waiting the coming of a Savior. They referred to Him as *Niskalanka Purusa*, the Sinless Man. We westerners include the Wise Men in our Christmas pageants, and sing *We Three Kings of Orient Are*, but we don't know much about them. Were there three? Where did they come from? Here in India, Christians are very sure who the Wise

Men were - they were Indians! They were sages who knew and understood the Vedas and were waiting for the Sinless Man to come. When Jesus was born, they worshiped Him as the Niskalanka Purusa.*

Like the Wise Men of old, we also seek truth, light and eternal life. Like the Wise Men of old, we also seek Him.

Blessed Season to you all!
The 4Smiths
(*Christ in Ancient Vedas by Joseph Padinjarekara.)

27 December 2002

Dear Mom and Dad,

Did you have a good Christmas? Ours revealed my selfish heart. Most of our Christian friends can't afford presents, so they celebrate by visiting in each others' homes, sharing food, enjoying the fire, and singing. It's nice, but it's different, especially for self-centered people like me who want to stay-at-home-open-presents-and-be-left-alone (I'm sorry, Lord). Our first visitors arrived at 9:00 am. I didn't handle it well. Learned later that we were lucky. Friends received their first visitors at 7:45! Sigh. I'm still learning to roll with the punches.

Isabel says thank you for the baby doll, but she does not like the doll's hat. She loves her own hats, but doesn't want one on the baby. If anybody puts the hat on, she proclaims, "No," and jerks it off. She won't put the doll down, either. So cute. Two months ago she only had one, but received so many for Christmas this year that her crib is full. She will only go to sleep if we line up all the babies right next to her. She knows when one is missing. She sits up, points at the pile and says, "Baby, baby," refusing to put her head down until they're all there. She and Eirene are so different. What would I do without them?

It's cold, but no snow, yet. We can see our breath in the kitchen. No one in the house is brave enough to take off all layers before putting on pj's and climbing into bed. When I realized it had been three days since I'd actually changed the bottom layer of my clothes, I knew I'd finally left image-conscious America behind.

Hugs from your not-quite-warm daughter,
Robin, for us all

18 January 2003

Dear Gramma Ruth and Grampa Bob,

I'm writing to tell you our big news - we're coming home in August! As of August 8, we will be home. For good? That's still unclear.

The saddest part of our decision concerns the house help. They've become part of our family. When we broke the news, one of the ladies said that her friends ask her why she walks all the way up here to the top of the Hill each day for work. She told them she doesn't feel like she's going to work. She's coming to spend time with her family. The girls greet the house help with big hugs each morning. The house help have taught them to speak Hindi. The love is real.

I'm learning to trust the Lord with the house help. I can try to shield them from sorrow, or I can let them walk through it, believing the Lord will meet them where they are. Maybe this all sounds funny. I mean, they're just employees, right? I'm not sure when it happened, but I love these ladies.

They are illiterate. They were married off at 15. They call me memsahib, and expect me to carry the responsibility of that role. For instance, when the cook was ill and in the hospital, it was understood that I would come and sit with her, and then speak to the doctor on her behalf. Her husband and eldest son couldn't understand much of what the doctor said, but all assumed I would know. I'm the memsahib!

I'm also learning to listen for God's still, small Voice in the midst of all the busyness. Living here has been the hardest thing we've ever done, and the best. We've grown and learned, and I know we still have a long way to go, but, we're so grateful for the time we've had here.

We recently put a bunk bed in the girls' room. Isabel had no trouble transitioning to it from her crib, probably because it's so cold. She snuggles under all her blankets and doesn't move until morning. When Isa was still in her crib, Eirene used to wake up first, climb down from her loft, and then join Isabel in the crib for playtime. Isabel was too little to clamber out when they were done, so one of us would have to go get her. The bunk bed has changed their routine. Now, Eirene climbs down from the top bunk, helps Isabel out from under her blankets, and then brings her into the warm living room. The first morning, here they came, blurry-eyed, wearing their footed-pajamas, Eirene leading Isabel by the hand, saying, "Mama, look what I found!"

I'll end with this - Isabel formed a 3-word sentence for the first time yesterday. She looked so cute in the sunglasses she was wearing that I told her to go show one of the staff. She did, then came waddling back like only toddlers can, announcing, "I did, Mama!"

I asked, "You did it?"

She repeated, "I did it," and then proceeded to run all over the house, yelling her new sentence. Your namesake couldn't be cuter.

Love,
Robin, for us all

25 February 2003

Hi Mom,

We miss you. Saying goodbye at the airport was devastating. We asked the taxi driver to wait just long enough for us to watch you walk through the front door, but he said the police would make him move, and drove away. As soon as Eirene felt the car begin to move, she started crying. I've never seen anything like it. The whole way on that long road from the airport she alternated between hysterically crying and putting her head down on Steve's shoulder. Every now and then, she'd sit up, put both hands on the car window in a pleading gesture, and cry, "Gramma! Gramma!" Steve and I thought our hearts would break right there in the car.

It wasn't until the next morning that it hit me you were really gone. We were on the train. I looked out the window and noticed a beautiful woman walking down the road. Beautiful, dark skin, bright lipstick, brightly colored sari. I almost turned to tell you to look out the window, when I remembered you weren't there.

Not that I mean to make you cry. Just trying to help you understand that even if we didn't do much while you were here, we loved how normal it felt to be together. Once we finally arrived home from Delhi, Isabel looked around, then said, "...Ama?" She kept it up for awhile, looking, asking and shrugging her shoulders until I finally told her you had gone bye-bye. She waved her little hand and said, "Bye-bye." You are loved and missed.

Thank you, too, for your comments about stress and our reactions to it. I thought about what you said all day Sunday, and I realized that I really do take my stress out on Steve in my mind, but the girls in practice. Yesterday, I praised Steve for something, and as soon as I said it I thought, *how long has it been since I praised Steve for something instead of teasing him for his failings?* I tease him about his forgetfulness. When was the last time I praised him for his intelligence? It was a sobering thought. Meanwhile, I take out my stress on the girls by being hard on them or frustrated by them. Too often, after dealing with all the issues of the day, here come the girls, and I think, *Can't you just behave so I don't have to deal with you, too?* Lord, forgive me.

We confessed to a friend last night that our marriage is more strained than ever, as are our relationships with the girls. It takes only very small things to shift us from everything's-fine-and-we-all-love-each-other to Awful. Our friend said that huge swings in emotion are common when living overseas. So nice to hear that this is also part of culture shock.

My fingers are about frozen. It hailed, rained and stormed just a couple of hours after we got back on Sunday. It stormed all night, and then was dark and cold all day Monday. Today, the sky is blue and the sun is warm, but the cold gets in my bones and doesn't leave. Steve is still convinced that being cold is better than being hot, but I'm not so sure. Remember, I was the one who moved away from Tahoe all those years ago! Who knew I'd marry a Southerner who was so tired of the heat that he'd pray to live somewhere cold?

Love to you,
Robin, for us all

28 February 2003
Dear Gramma Ruth and Grampa Bob,

Mom has left, so I finally have time to write you about our trip to Thailand. How can I describe the freedom found in exchanging this mountain clothing for swimsuits and flip flops? Indian clothing is very conservative. Even on warm days, I rarely let my ankles show. The local dress consists of a matching tunic and pants, plus a scarf worn "backwards," with the tassels hanging down the back instead of the front. Today, I am wearing long johns, wool socks, and a wool turtleneck underneath the local outfit, and another sweater over all. Thailand's warm sun shocked our too-white skin.

We hated saying goodbye to Dad, but were so grateful to have Mom return with us to the mountains. Eirene and Isabel loved sharing their room with her. Most mornings, the girls crawled out of their bunk bed and climbed straight up the ladder to read with her in the loft. The goodbye at the airport was horrible.

One day, Mom asked, "Don't you have any grocery stores here?"

I looked at her blankly for a second, then said, "Well, no, I guess not." There are no grocery stores here, not even in the capital city of Delhi. Every now and then, we'll find a store about the size of a 7-

Eleven, but nothing larger. Instead, streets are lined with vegetable carts and small shops carrying anything and everything. One shop near us sells both hand-made sweaters and medicine. Another provides dry cleaning and a booth for international phone calls.

Mom's question got me thinking. Steve and I don't ask *why* as often as we used to. Why don't Indians form lines at counters? Why don't the cars have defrost? Why do they think that all white foreigners are rich? We were told that why questions decrease in the more advanced stages of culture shock. It's nice to no longer be surprised by what we see, but sadly, we still judge what we see. Unfortunately, many missionaries leave their field of service without pushing through these final stages of culture shock. They take these negative feelings back home with them. We're praying for the grace to push through these stages so that once we're home again, we can remember this place and these people with love, compassion, and appreciation, not judgment.

Your (hopefully) less judgmental granddaughter,
Robin

13 March 2003
Hi, Mom,

I have typhoid. Ugh! No one told us that typhoid immunizations are only 60% effective. The doctor thinks that I've had it for about a week. There are three stages. First, there's headache, runny nose, and cough. Then, tummy troubles which is where I am now (oh joy). The third stage is bad and long-term, but the meds I'm taking will prevent it.

I'm not quarantined, but I have to wash my hands every chance I get. The girls are fine. I'm utterly exhausted but not sleepy, so I get bored easily. After resting a while, I try to be useful by doing laundry or something, but then become worn out and lie down, until it's time to go to the toilet again. And again.

I'll call or write more when I have more energy.

Love you both,
Robin, for us all

About the time I was diagnosed with typhoid, America declared war on Iraq. The whole world was watching the Middle East, but our little corner of the world felt isolated from it all.

25 March 2003

Hey Mom and Dad,

Steve here. I stayed with Robin last night at the hospital. She wants to come home, but the doctors said not yet. Essentially, they think two things. First, she still has typhoid, though it's under control and diminishing. Second, she seems to have a mass of some sort, amoebas and maybe also bacteria, traveling through her intestines.

Over the past six months, Robin has suffered significant abdominal pain whenever she's had tummy troubles. Often the pain lingered even after the other symptoms disappeared. The doctors think that the medicines she's taken these past months for all the various (mostly minor) stomach problems have kept the mass from growing too large, but never totally destroyed it, either. Thus, they want to keep her for another 24 hours to really attack this mass with anti-amoeba and antibiotic treatments through IV. The doctor said they are "shooting the cannons" at this thing now, and Robin should feel better soon.

Love you both!
Steve
PS: The girls have been fine at the house without us. The interns and house help are taking good care of them.

26 March 2003

Dear Mom and Dad,

I write to you from the hospital bed. For the record, I am feeling much better. Thank you for your prayers! I get to go home today!

It's 5 am. The night-duty nurse just took my temperature and blood pressure. The nurses here are very sweet, and are happy to see me doing so much better. Most of them have not received formal training, but instead have completed apprenticeship here at the hospital, so while they aren't as professional as their western counterparts, they are kind and try to make me comfortable. They still wear those old-fashioned nurse caps that you see in old movies, but I guess that's appropriate, considering that I'm lying in a bed that was made in about 1917.

Remember how much I loved reading the *Madeline* books when I was little? In the first story Madeline is rushed to the hospital to get her appendix taken out. The bed frame is iron, and there's a handle for raising and lowering it. I think the line goes *and on her bed, there was a crank*. That's what I'm sleeping in. My IV hangs on a wooden stand with no wheels next to my bed. It's about 6 feet high and very heavy. Steve carries the pole when I have to go to the bathroom.

The bed pans here are the old-fashioned, cast iron-enamel things you see on old episodes of MASH. None of the rooms have TVs or phones. To make a call, I have to go down to the receptionist desk on the ground floor, and the only way to get there is the stairs. No elevator. There is one wheelchair, but it doesn't roll smoothly. The only people who use it are my girls. They play on it when they come to visit. How do patients get up to the operating theatre (operation room) on the first floor (American second floor) you ask? The patient sits in a chair that has four longs handles. The four strongest staff members who happen to be around at the time then pick up the chair and carry the patient up the stairs. I know because they did it for me last year when I hurt my ankle. I hated every second of it. The guys were different heights and they took the stairs at different times.

I can't help but laugh when I remember how shocked we were during our first overnight stay 18 months ago when Eirene had pneumonia. Old room. Dirty, cement floor. No toilet paper in the bathroom. Thoughtful but under-trained nurses. This visit, I didn't think twice about slipping between these musty sheets! Absolutely, my standards have lowered, but also, I'm learning to be grateful. Most people in this nation don't have access even to something as old fashioned as our hospital. How can I complain about a less-than-perfectly-scrubbed hospital room when it's staffed by doctors and nurses we trust?

So, that was a little tour of my world. It is surreal to hear people talking on their mobile phones in a corridor that hasn't changed since WW1. Or, for that matter, typing on a lap-top while lying on a bed with a crank. I wouldn't want to be treated anywhere else.

It is gross to learn I've had a mass of amoebae in my intestines for a long time. The doctors could actually feel the floating "mass" (their word) during the initial examination. Oh, let's not talk about it...

I've been memorizing Deuteronomy 8:2-5. Lying here gives me plenty of time to repeat it to myself. Here's how it goes:

> Remember how the Lord your God carried you all the way
> in the desert these forty years, to humble you and to test
> you, in order to know what was in your hearts, whether or
> not you would keep His commands. He humbled you,
> causing you to hunger, and then feeding you with manna,
> which neither you nor your fathers had known to teach you

that man does not live on bread alone, but on every word that comes from the mouth of the Lord. Your clothes did not wear out and your feet did not swell in all these forty years. Know then in your heart, that as a man disciplines his son, so the Lord your God disciplines you.

When I first started memorizing the passage, I got upset. OK, so we've lived in India less than two years, and we're in the mountains, not the desert, but still! Their feet never got swollen in forty years of wandering in the desert? One or the other of us Smiths has been sick since we got here. *What's the deal, Lord?*

He answered my question pretty quickly, "Robin, you eat ice-cream. You have a TV. You sleep in a bed. You have a bathroom. They slept in tents on sand and had no food except what I gave them. I tested them in some things, and gave them grace in others (no swollen feet). Likewise, I've tested you in some things - sickness - and given you grace in others."

As soon as I thought those words, I began to count the ways God has been good to us these two years. He's given us so much! Later that very day, I ended up in the hospital again.

Here in this musty, dirty room, lying on this old, hard bed, I've had nothing else to do but meditate on the fact that God has held us and sustained us these many months. He has carried us through this desert, and now, we, too, are standing at the edge of the land. We are moving home in several months, and God's hand of provision will be less obvious. We won't suffer from typhoid and dysentery once we get back to Austin. There will be hot showers, kid-friendly restaurants, drinkable water. Additionally, here in India, we live on support. If Steve gets his old job back in the corporate world, will we be tempted to think that the money he earns is "our" money? My prayer these last two days has been, "Oh, Lord, please don't let us fall into the illusion of self-sufficiency! May the lessons we've learned here in this desert not only remain with us, but grow in our hearts, as we return to the west."

I have felt your prayers as I've lain in this bed. More than ever, I'm so very grateful for you both. I can't wait to see you this summer!

Love,
Robin

31 March 2003

Dear Mom and Dad,

I've been thinking lately about why India, with all her vast resources of people and goods, is such a mess. Yes, sometimes, I still ask that why question. Why so much trash? Why don't people just stop littering? Why is it that in 2003, the gutter is still most people's toilet?

We've been learning about caste. Hindus believe they are born into a caste. To reincarnate to a higher caste in the next life, they must accept the fate that's been handed to them in this life. If they are born into a caste of toilet cleaners or street sweepers, they must not question or be discontent, but must do their duty faithfully, and hope for an upgrade in the next life. Caste affects everything. For instance, why do Indians litter? Why not? The street sweepers will clean it. They must.

Guidebooks state that India abolished caste 50 years ago. It's complicated. Think about it this way - America is 250 years old. If someone took over and declared the Bill of Rights null and void, would we go along with it? Of course not. We'd probably cling to our rights more fiercely. Compared to caste, our history is short. Caste has been around for thousands of years. Governmental policies matter little compared to such ingrained tradition.

Please keep praying for the peoples of India, that they would see there is an Option to the hopelessness of caste and karma. Pray for us, too, that we never forget how hopeless life is without Him.

We love you,
Robin, for us all

28 April 2003

Dear Mom and Dad,

Steve is at the hospital. He spent most of the night in the bathroom due to tummy issues. The power was out due to a storm, though, so the poor guy had to stumble in the pitch-black with a rumbling belly. Pray for him. Pray for all of us. I was on medicine all last week for similar issues, and still don't seem to be over it. Isabel has had some nasty diapers for about a week. Now, even Eirene seems to be hit. For two days, we've heard, "Mommy, my stomach hurts," and then watched her run for the bathroom. Ah, the glamour of the missionary life!

These tummy issues never seem to end. We try to do the right things. We drink clean water, don't eat at questionable places, shower with our mouths closed, and wash our vegetables in iodine before we cook them. Even our doctors think that we seem to have it rougher than most, something I say with no pride in my heart. Sickness is not a badge of honor (or martyrdom). It just seems to be a part of our story. Other people have different stories. God is the Author of all.

In other news, Isabel had a lovely second birthday. She is everyone's delight. Eirene isn't jealous of her limelight, either. Their friendship amazes us. Eirene is loving the preschool she's attending. Our pastor's wife just opened it this semester. There are seven students - five Indians and three foreigners, including Eirene. Instruction is in English, but the children speak Hindi on the playground. Among other things, Eirene has learned some Hindi worship songs, the Hindi alphabet (49 letters!), and that cricket is a really fun game.

Finally, if you emailed us recently, I probably didn't get it. Our phones were down most of last week due to two unrelated events. First, the phone company was upgrading to computers. Somewhere along the way, all records were lost. Seems they figured the easiest solution was to cut everyone's line, thereby forcing people to come to the office with their most recent bills to prove they'd paid. Second, in the midst of all that chaos, a street sweeper was sweeping leaves off the street one day, but then set fire to his leaf pile a little too close to the phone lines and burned them!

Love from this crazy, wonderful place,
Robin, for us all

25 May 2003

Hi Mom and Dad,

I have good news and bad. First, the good news: the couple who were going to replace us in August are expecting their first child. They'd been trying for a while, so are thrilled and excited. Baby is due in December. The bad news is that their home church has decided not to support them financially after August. It's now probable that they will leave permanently in August. If they do, Steve and I are considering staying for another 6 - 12 months. There are several reasons for this, not the least of which is that our hearts have softened toward this place over the last two months. Please call if you want to talk, at whatever time is convenient for you, even if it's our night.

We love you and are praying for God's outcome, whatever that might be.

Love,
Robin, for us all

21 June 2003

Dear Mom and Dad,

It's official! Our time in India is not finished. Before I go any farther, though, here's a promise:

Living in this house on a long-term basis is not the best thing for our family. Our attentions are divided between the girls and 10-20 other people all the time. We have no intention of extending our stay now, then again and again until, before we know it, five years have gone by without a real plan or vision. Also, though Steve is good at what he does, engineering is not his passion. If we were ever going to live in India long-term, it would have to be for more than mentoring western interns or the construction of buildings.

Now, our hearts:

C.S. Lewis once explained that for God to be truly God, He must be both perfect and personal. Perfection is necessary because only a perfect God, one who is above and beyond human struggles, has the answers we need. However, perfection isn't enough. God must also be personal. A perfect God who knows the answers but can't communicate them is pretty useless. Steve and I know you and Dad agree wholeheartedly with these points. I remind you of them today because of what I read in the *Hindustan Times* on Thursday, June 5:

> Those [Hindu gods] we...worshiped [in times past] were never really heroic in the western sense. They were vulnerable. They were playful. They occasionally – in fact, frequently – did wrong. They were just like you and me: entirely human. So were our villains. They often rose above themselves to acquire heroic proportions. That is why good and bad always went hand in hand in our epics. They were never in conflict. They cohabited, as in life.
>
> Since everything was illusory, so was truth. And since truth did not exist, nor did falsehood. While people occasionally deviated from the facts, no one ever lied...in our society, decisiveness was never a virtue. It [decisiveness] ...revealed an appalling lack of maturity and wisdom. Our

heroes spoke with forked tongues. It was not a sign of
deceit, but of wisdom...

Speaking with a forked tongue is wise, not deceitful. There is no
perfect God. *There are no decisive answers.* In the last six months, our
hearts have softened toward this place. What used to drive us crazy
now drives us to our knees. Editorials such as this astonish, perplex and
break us. We can't leave. Not yet.

For the sake of the Personal, Perfect God,
Robin, Steve and the girls

29 August 2003

Dear Mom and Dad,

What an absolutely wonderful visit. We miss you already, but
treasure the memories we made over the last few weeks with you in
Austin. Now, here we are, "home" again in this drafty old house, safe
and sound.

The girls are thrilled to be back. Eirene even attended school
yesterday. Due to jet lag, she woke up early. At 5 am, she was already
asking what we were going to do all day. We'd been home less than 24
hours, but when I suggested school, she jumped up, got dressed and
fixed a snack. She packed her backpack and put it on, ready to go.
Unfortunately, it was only 6:00. When she heard that she couldn't leave
for two more hours, she didn't care. She wore that backpack all
morning. Later, Isabel wouldn't leave her auntie's side. At one point,
they were on the floor playing, but Isabel was getting tired, so she laid
down and used her Auntie's leg as a pillow.

It is wet. People are calling this the best monsoon in years. The
clouds sit on us for hours, turning our whole world gray. Everything is
wet - walls, books, our clothes. And there is mold. It's growing on my
boots. This is no mere light dusting of white powder sometimes called
mold. This stuff is bright green and thick as a carpet. The caulking on
the windows has sprouted moss. The front walkway is so slick from
moss that the girls have to hold our hands when walking down to the
car. Ah, home!

New interns arrive on Tuesday. We'll issue familiar warnings:
No, you cannot drink the water. No, you may not wear shorts on warm
days. No, you must absolutely not put toilet paper into the toilet.
Finally, yes, we mean it when we say "On days with no water delivery, if
it's 'yellow,' let it mellow." Then, Steve will be in Bangladesh for 16 days

next month. It's good to be back!

Love,
Robin and all

6 September 2003
Dear Mom and Dad,

So, I brought back three cans of cream of mushroom soup for special meals during the holidays. I showed them to the interns. Explained how they are not to touch these cans because I am saving them. That was eight days ago. Two cans are already gone. I ask you, who would need my soup so badly?

Your perplexed daughter,
Robin

24 September 2003
DearMom and Dad,

I have just a minute to write before heading off to see the doctor. The meds I took last week don't seem to have done the trick. It's a minor issue, though. The Lord is covering us girls with great grace during Steve's trip to Bangladesh. Thanks for your prayers!

In the past two weeks, I've had conversations with three missionary wives. All of them are going through tough times right now, and each opened up to me in unexpected times and places. Astounding. I have nothing to offer. These women are older than I, have been married longer, and two have even served on the field longer, yet they've opened up to me? Being a clay pot used by the Living God is rather wonderful.

God is faithful. Spread the word!
Robin, for us all

28 September 2003
Dear Mom and Dad,

Rain. Fog. Rain. Shafts of sunlight breaking through clouds. Hello's. Goodbye's. There you have it - our first month back in India.

Yes, it is still raining. Every now and then, a ray of sunshine shoots through the clouds and makes us wonder if perhaps this will be the day it ends, but always the clouds return.

Steve is still gone on his project trip. Sometimes, I think about how many days there are still to go, worry how I'll fill the weekend with activities, or dread the approach of Sunday and walking the girls down the hill to the worship service on my own. Those moments are overwhelming. Then I remember Jesus' words about not worrying about tomorrow, and I determine to live in this day (or hour or minute), and, just as He promised, He's faithfully seeing us through, one day at a time.

Steve and his team aren't the only ones absent. Everyone else is on a project trip in south India. A pastor there needs a chapel designed. Tragically, he and wife lost their 10-year-old son last year in an accident. They had recently given him permission to walk home alone from the bus stop (a distance of about one block), but one day he didn't come home. The parents called the school. The bus driver said he dropped the boy at his stop. The parents went searching the street. After a couple of hours, they found their son's body in some bushes. He'd been hit by a car, but no one stopped to help. There were skid marks on the road, but no indication the car had bothered to stop. Shop owners all admitted to having heard a commotion, but none came out to investigate. This couple had a baby after their son died, so they are busy with two at home, but their joy is bittersweet.

Rain. Fog. Shafts of sunlight breaking through clouds. Exciting hello's. Permanent and devastating goodbye's. Life is hard. I pray that Peter was right - *...for a little while [we] may have to suffer trials of many kinds, yet trusting in Him now without seeing Him, [we] are filled with a glorious joy too great for words* (1 Peter 1:6-9).

I love you,
Robin and the girls (and Steve)

The following is an email I wrote to a potential new family:
27 October 2003
Dear T,

As far as travel experience goes, Steve had very little when we moved here. Before marrying me, his biggest move was from Louisiana to Texas for college. He spent one summer in California during his college years and participated in a 2-week mission trip to Ukraine, but that was it. On the other hand, when I was growing up, my family moved every four years, including a 3-year stint overseas. I lived in Norway for one semester during college. My family is spread out all over, and we visit each other often. During our first year of marriage,

Steve traveled more than he had in his whole life. Sure, having travel experience is helpful, but when the Lord calls, He gives grace. Really, really.

Sickness. We've had our share. Within months of our arrival in 2001, both our girls were hospitalized with pneumonia. Isabel had two serious UTIs before her first birthday. We've all had dysentery more times than we can count. The girls are just now getting over chicken pox. On the other hand, we have friends who rarely get sick. Others might get dysentery only occasionally. For us, being ill has been part of our lives here. At first we couldn't believe it, but then we learned the routine at the hospital and got used to being the Bearer of Stool Samples.

Not that it's been easy. When we first arrived, all we knew was that we wanted God to work in us. We never imagined He'd use illness to do it. We've been angry. Depressed. We've even been afraid of God, wondering what other lessons He had in store. So many misconceptions both about Him and life have come to the surface because of and through the illnesses. There are even days I'm grateful we've been ill because through it all we have personally experienced His grace. It really is abundant. We are *learning to be content in any circumstance*, a phrase I used to hate but now love because of that wonderful word learned. Paul had to learn to be content. In other words, there were times when he wasn't. There were probably times when he wished he didn't have to go through what he was going through. I now know (in a very small way) why Job questioned God, and I also know (in a very small way) why God responded to him with a poem about His own sovereignty. Steve and I have heard that very same response to our questions and fears.

If you move here, you'll probably get sick. Only the Lord knows. If you do get sick, God will see you through. And your children. We've had to trust God with our kids time and again during the past two+ years. I pray we forever hold our children lightly before the Lord because of what we've learned here. On the very practical side, medicine is cheaper here than any other country I know. That makes the lessons easier to take!

Travel. It's a long trip. India is far away. I'm not sure what else to say except that God gives grace. When I was pregnant with Isabel, our 18-month-old and I traveled alone to meet Steve who was already here on a project trip. Our tickets were booked on a flight that originated in Houston, not Austin (our hometown). My parents drove Eirene and me the 3-hours to the Houston airport. We hugged them goodbye and got on the plane. The doors closed. Then, nothing. The plane didn't move. Four hours later, they opened the doors, and we all - the whole planeload - got off. We'd gone nowhere. A light in the cockpit that was supposed to turn off, wouldn't, so we couldn't take off. We sat on that plane for four hours. No food. No in-flight movie. We spent the night in the airport hotel, then boarded another plane the next day. We were 24 hours into our trip and hadn't even left Texas! The second plane took us to London where we endured a 12-hour layover. Finally, we boarded a plane for India. In Delhi, we rested at a hotel for three hours, then boarded a train. Four hours after that, we got in a taxi. Two hours later, we transferred from the taxi to a jeep, and drove the last hour up the Hill to the mission. Three days later, we turned around and went back home again. Crazy, right? Thing is, I wouldn't have dreamed of not coming. I laugh as I look back on that trip. It's unbelievable we did all that for a 3-day stay, but it was the right thing for us, so the Lord gave us grace.

Airlines have since installed individual televisions for each passenger. We now watch movies the entire flight without apology. Even without them though, the only thing to say about travel is what's already been said - God will get you through. If it seems scary and more than you can handle, then know it's the perfect opportunity for Him to prove His own abilities. Finally, in the end, if your fears are realized and the kids misbehave, no one sleeps and your fellow passengers hate you for nine hours, oh well. That, too, shall pass and you'll have your own great story to tell!

Blessings on you guys as you pursue Him,
Robin, for us all

3 November 2003

Dear Mom and Dad,

I've been reading a lot lately. It happens when you have typhoid. Technically, without a blood test I cannot say conclusively that this is typhoid again, but all the symptoms are there. I'm exhausted, but tired of sleeping, so I've been reading. And reading. May I share with you very quickly something I read today? It's from Max Lucado's *No Wonder They Call Him the Savior*:

> ...I've always perceived John (the Apostle) as a fellow
> who viewed life simply....For example, defining Jesus [is] a
> challenge to the best of writers, but John handles the task

with casual analogy. The Messiah, in a word, was "the Word." A walking message. A love letter...

But I like John most for the way he loved Jesus...John is the only one of the twelve (original apostles) who was at the cross...By his own admission, he hadn't quite put the pieces together yet. But that didn't really matter. As far as he was concerned, his closest Friend was in trouble and he came to help.

"Can you take care of My mother?" (Jesus asked him from the cross.) Of course. That's what friends are for....John teaches us that the strongest relationship with Christ may not necessarily be a complicated one...The greatest webs of loyalty are spun, not with airtight theologies or foolproof philosophies, but with friendships: stubborn, selfless, joyful friendships.

Living in India has helped us see what John knew- strong friendship with Jesus is more important than perfect theology.

Two weeks ago, one million people here in North India followed behind one man (one!) as he walked on pilgrimage from one city to another. Authorities had to close down cities in order to manage the crowds. He claims to have a personal key to God, a verbal message that supposedly gets God's attention every time. One million people are hoping he's right.

India. Smelly. Dirty. Crowded. Confusing. Home to countless numbers of people who are desperate to know how to reach God, to make sure He's paying attention. They are desperate to discover what John knew: God is our Friend. As I lie here in this bed this week, I'm echoing a prayer you often pray - May the god-man those one million people are following inadvertently lead them to the Only God Who Is. May the seekers find.

Love,
Robin, for us all

4 December 2003
Dear Mom and Dad,

Today, a man from the Central Bureau (similar to our FBI) came to our front door. He wanted to know what it is, exactly, that we do here? Are we converting people?

We invited him to come in from the crisp December day. We

seated him by the buchari. Our cook made chai. He enjoyed it with some cookies. Then came the questions. Who are we? How long have we been here? What do we do, exactly? May he see an example of our architecture and/or engineering work? May he see our passports and visas?

Finally, he left after making a list of everyone's names, including the Indian staff. He wanted to know their names, their fathers' names, and their religions. Several states in India have anti-conversion laws that state no one is allowed to coerce or entice someone into changing religions. Unfortunately, in a country where many people are starving, the simple act of giving free food to a beggar can be (and has been) considered coercion. We're curious to know how this man came to be at our door. The only explanation is that someone must have reported we are engaging in coercion.

Who would report such a lie? There are a couple of possibilities, the most obvious being the man who is in litigation right now with our landlord. It would have been easy for him to breathe a word into the right person's ear in hopes that we'd have to leave. We'll probably never know.

In the end, it was a fine visit. We have nothing to hide. The man was impressed by all the work going on, but in the end was most interested to talk with our Indian/American couple. He asked the Indian husband, "What's it like being married to an American?"

He's gone. We're fine. Reeling a bit from the unexpected, but that's all. I love that God is never faced by something unexpected. He's never overwhelmed by our experiences. He never gets tired, never feels jet-lag. He watches and tends to us here, while also watching and tending you in America. He's so big. So able. So God. After living here, I now know that I'll never fully understand Him or His ways. He doesn't expect me to. What He wants is for me to trust Him. I think I'm finally starting to.

Loving you,
Robin, for us all

17 December 2003
Dear Grandma Ruth and Grandpa Bob,

Thank you for Eirene's package. Her birthday isn't until next Monday, but we're having a party for her this week, due to next week's travels. Did my dad tell you we're going to Goa for Christmas? Sun! Ocean! Is surreal to pack swimsuits when I can see my breath outside, and the office feels like a fridge.

Eirene's super excited about her party. Like the rest of our lives, her day will be both American and Indian. People will speak Hindi and English. Some will wear western clothes; others Indian. We'll eat both American food and Indian.

Eirene has studied Hindi at school for the last year, and now knows the Hindi alphabet better than I. Last week when we needed to dress nicely for an event, she asked if she could wear Indian clothes like other girls her age. That was a first. Meanwhile, Isabel does pretty well with Hindi, too. The house help speak to her in Hindi, and though she seldom answers back, she understands perfectly. It makes me sad that they will lose these things.

I hope we don't lose the lessons we've learned. I don't want to start buying clothes I don't need or shoes to match every outfit. There are more important things than immaculate lawns and perfectly decorated homes. Before we moved here, I taped electrical cords out of the way so that no one had to see unsightly cords in my house. I thought it mattered. Wouldn't you know it, the first thing I noticed when we moved into this house was the thick, jet-black, cable TV cord running right up the wall and out the only window in the living room. Only the Lord could bring me to the other side of the world to teach me a lesson I didn't know I needed. I hated that cord. Finally, the day came when I realized it just didn't matter. Who cares??!!?? And so, we mature. Slowly, but surely. Thanks be to the Father, Son and Spirit!

Love,
Robin, for us all

1 January 2004

Happy New Year, Mom and Dad!

I'm getting nervous about our return. We have to figure out where we're going to live, buy beds and cars, readjust to only seating four people around the dinner table again, and...and...

Steve and I are fasting this week to start our new year. The best way to get our minds right is by choosing to focus on God, so we're fasting. Can I say that I dislike it? I hate feeling hungry. I'm desperate for God to give grace to do this thing, hoping He will accept my hunger as prayer. I'm also grateful that, in reality, everything is in His hands whether I acknowledge it or not.

You mean the world to us,
Robin, for us all

4 January 2004

Hey Mom and Dad,

The girls wore matching outfits to church this morning, and didn't take off a single layer during the whole service: two pairs of leggings, wool dress, sweater, coat, mittens and hat. They would have been warmer standing outside in the sun on this cold, January day than sitting inside for the worship the service. These old homes have such thick cement walls and no central heat. The sun can't penetrate. This is our third winter, but I'm still adjusting to the local logic - go outside to warm up in the winter.

About 10 minutes into the service, none of us could feel our toes. The band was rocking, so some of us started jumping to the beat. I'm afraid it was more about survival than actual worship.

Crazy place. How crazy are we that we like it?

Love,
Robin, for us all

10 January 2004

Dear Mom and Dad,

We'll be coming home soon. Will it feel like home? Will Steve feel comfortable in his cubicle back at his old job after 2 1/2 years of working in the midst of power outages, disconnected phones, and smoky wood burning stoves? It's almost time to move out of our comfort zones again. Not that we're always comfortable here in the subcontinent. Take our recent return from sun-kissed, laid-back Goa. It was so relaxing in the sand and surf that we kind of forgot we were in India. Then, we stepped off the train in Delhi. Usually we're prepared. Even before the train comes to a full stop, we're steeling ourselves against the onslaught of taxi drivers, auto-rickshaw drivers, and beggars who work the platforms of the station. This time, our defenses were down due to the holiday so that when we disembarked, we felt like (and looked like) newcomers. A small crowd surrounded us. Two taxi drivers started fighting each other over who would get us.

There are twelve platforms at the Delhi station. We weren't sure which one we were on, so we looked around for the sign. Not a good move. We must be tourists! More people surrounded us. What's most frustrating is that no one just helps. Everyone has an agenda. We finally made it to what we thought was the right platform for the final ride home, but, weren't quite sure. Decided that Isabel and I would stay with the luggage while Steve and Eirene ran all the way back to the other side of the station to check the one information board.

An elevated walkway crosses over all the tracks. Even on a normal day, the Delhi station is super crowded, but that day the trains were running late due to heavy fog so that walkway was mobbed. Coolies (porters) with suitcases on their heads rushing to catch trains. Travelers shoving through to keep up with their coolies. Then, Steve realized that up ahead, half of the walkway was cordoned off for construction. The throng was pushing through that narrow section like sand swirling down a funnel. He had to either join the flow or get trampled. Steve picked up Eirene to keep her safe, then shoved for all he was worth. By the time they got to the other side, the pickpocket had struck. The crush of people had been the perfect opportunity for someone to (1) undo the Velcro flap over Steve's pocket, (2) open the zipper, and (3) pull out his wallet. Steve never felt a thing. That Jesus felt the *power leave Him* when the woman with the issue of blood touched Him was miraculous. No wonder the disciples were astonished and said, *"Look at the crowd pressing around You. How can You ask, 'Who touched Me?'"*

Pickpockets. Foreigners make prime targets. The many policemen who patrol the station turn a blind eye for a portion of the take.

Thankfully, most of our money wasn't in the wallet, and we were able to cancel the credit cards quickly, but this was the third time in seven months that we've been robbed. We are not lax. We take precautions. They are relentless in their pursuit. They watch and follow us from the time we get off the train or out of the taxi until we get on the next train or enter the airport, and three times we've looked the wrong way, paused one second too long, or been stuck in the wrong mass of people. How disappointed we've been! How angry! This time felt no different. We were livid when we boarded that last train, wanted to run away, to finally give in to hate and anger. Then we realized that all those people - the pickpockets, the policemen with greased palms, the taxi drivers fighting over foreigners - they're all trapped in darkness. It's so sad. If we, proud and judgmental as we are, can now have hearts which break for India, how much more must the heart of God!

We only have a few weeks left. We leave today on our last project trip. By train. Hoards of travelers. Naked beggars trying to survive the winter. Scam artists. Starving children. Pickpockets. Will you pray for India during our trip? We will pass, literally, thousands of people as we travel. It boggles the mind to think that God knows the name of each one. Each is precious to Him! Pray that they will come to know God and His light. Pray that we'll learn to love them more.

Looking forward to seeing you soon!
Robin, for us all

26 January 2004
Dear Mom and Dad,

It's done. The last project trip. Thank you for your prayers. I wrote the following email during the trip, but was unable to send it. Though the news is now old, I knew you'd want to hear it.

...The weather here is beautiful, complete with cool mornings and evenings, but warm afternoons. The terrain is the prettiest we've seen, except for our beloved Himalayas. Fields surround the home where we're staying. The flat roof feels positively biblical. I now understand the story of the men who lowered their sick friend to Jesus through the roof. The girls love to play up here. It's also the perfect spot from which to see the sights: village children walking to school, men in *longhis* (wrap-around skirts) on their bicycles, meandering cows looking for food, stray dogs. The women's saris are so bright - hues of red, blue and green that we westerners would never wear. From up here, they are like dots of color painted onto brown canvas.

Our train left Delhi at 4:30 pm on a Tuesday. We expected to reach our destination around 10:00 the next morning. However, due to heavy fog and "agitation on the tracks" (freedom fighters protesting something), we arrived seven hours late. Not unusual, right? Trains here often run late. That l.o.n.g trip was unique, though. Our train car was, essentially, empty. Besides our team, there were only three other people on that car. Three!!! Privacy is nonexistent in a country of almost a billion people, yet, for 24 hours we reveled in both space and quiet. God is kind.

On the other hand, the local pastor had to wait at the station for seven hours. There are always two sides, aren't there? We disembarked, followed the man to his jeep on shaky legs, and began the six hour, 170 km drive to his property. We were so glad to finally get off that train, but now we were bouncing, dodging and threading our way between giant potholes, and past over-loaded trucks and villagers on bicycles. Then the sun set. No street lights. Now we were dodging bicycles in the dark. We finally arrived about 10:00 pm, just in time for dinner. In case you've ever wondered, you now know how to get to the middle of nowhere.

One million villagers and subsistence, hand-to-mouth farmers live in this area without a single hospital to serve them. The local pastor has shared story after story of villagers who have died due to snake bites, accident and disease because there's no way to get help. We are here to design a hospital he will build on his property. It's wonderful to put our hands to something that is so needed.

So there you have it - a glimpse of our last Indian road trip. Thank you for your prayers. Hard to believe it's almost over.

Love,
Robin, for us all

2 February 2004

Dear Mom and Dad,

Here is is, the first of February, and we've already had more snow than all last year. It's as cloudy as monsoon season, too, so we don't see the sun for days at a time. Cabin fever has set in. We can see our breath in every room without a buchari, so our days consist of running to the bedroom to get a toy or schoolwork, and then back to the living room to play with it or work on it. Never again will I imagine scenes from *Little House on the Prairie* to be quaint and romantic. Laura Ingalls was cold!

I'm still surprised when there is thunder and lightning during snow storms. Isn't snow supposed to fall quietly? During a storm the other night, a bolt of electricity leapt out of a wall socket! We heard a loud pop after that, then the sound of glass breaking. One of the light bulbs exploded from the surge.

We haven't attended a worship service for weeks. It's been too hard to even think about walking all the way down in the snow just to sit in that cold building for two hours, and then to walk home again. Uphill. I've tried to not feel guilty about just "doing" church here at home. Being sick hasn't helped. I was hit with a sinus infection and tonsillitis right before the project trip. During the trip, it got pretty bad. I didn't mention it in my email because I wanted to focus on positives for a change. The whole truth about the trip is that one morning, the sinus pain made me into a blubbering mess. Those wonderful people kept saying, "Don't worry, it'll be all right" in Hindi. All I could do was respond with a little smile that I'm sure looked more like a grimace. The team doctor prescribed some meds which helped, but by the time we got back home, I felt as bad as ever. It seems the prescription was right, just not long enough.

The other night Steve and I slept on a mattress in the living room next to the buchari. We couldn't take the thought of leaving the warm living room to go sleep in our freezing bedroom. I lay there, thankful to be warm, but with painful head and ears. My glands were swollen. Mouth was dry. Then, cramps. Giardia. Again. I cried out to God (rather pitifully I'm afraid) to please just let me get through the night without throwing up. Hugging the porcelain in that freezing bathroom all night would have pushed me over the edge.

About 3:00 am, the power went out, so here came Eirene, scared because of the dark (and the lightning!), asking to crawl into bed with us. We were sleeping on an extra-wide twin mattress. Eirene sleeps like any good 5-year-old, all over the place. God loves giving us good stories to tell. Thankfully, I did end up with good meds and my sinuses right now are better than they've been in weeks. There will be no plugged ears on the plane ride home!

One of the lady interns is ill. She's sleeping in our bed at the moment. Steve and I will take her to the hospital this afternoon. Eirene and Isabel are so bored that they want to come, too. Is it just me, or is it strange that going to the hospital is our fun, family outing for the day?

Hope this hasn't been too depressing. We're actually feeling encouraged these days. God is just so good. We're beginning to see how He's used everything from the past two+ years to make us more like Him. Sickness. Loneliness. Busyness. Communal living. He owes us nothing, but He's taking the time to show us bits and pieces of the "why" for all of them. We are in awe. Soon, very soon, we'll be together and I'll tell you all about it.

Love you both,
Robin, for us all

8 February 2004
Dear Mom and Dad,

We've been reading Job lately and have come to a conclusion. His story is not about suffering. It's about faith. Will a man trust God even though everything in life indicates he shouldn't? No, Steve and I cannot compare our experiences with Job's. At all. What we can say is that through our very small trials, we have also come to realize that God is worth believing in. He is worth trusting, even though bad things happen. I hope such lessons will continue for the rest of our lives.

We bought tickets! Our plane leaves at 3 am on Feb 24. Good thing, too, because our visa expires at midnight on Feb 23. We will have to cross immigration before midnight. Keeping your granddaughters busy from midnight to 3 am will be interesting. We know you'll be praying.

We love you. Always.
Robin, for us all

17 February 2004
Dear Mom and Dad,

Two and a half years ago, we reported, "We're here." Now the time has come for, what? A final thought? A quick, farewell hug? Saying goodbye to our Indian family is wrenching our hearts. They held us up, both physically and spiritually, through the last years' frustrations, confusions, anger and joy. It would be easier to rush through the goodbyes, to not cry until we get on the plane, but we don't want to pretend. The Bible promises that those who mourn are *blessed, for they shall be comforted*. We're trying to embrace God in the sadness instead of pretending this isn't sad. He is here. We feel Him in each goodbye.

Oh the wonder of Heaven, where we will never have to say goodbye ever again!

For Him with you, Mom and Dad,
Robin and all

27 February 2004
Dear India Family,

Hello, One and All! Greetings from Austin, Texas. We are back home, though now we know more than ever that God is our Home.

We miss you.

It's 4:30 in the morning. I've already been up for two hours, but none of you need me to describe jet-lag. Thankfully, the girls are sleeping. Two nights ago, Isabel woke us about 3 am by yelling out that she was "...done sleeping." Thirty minutes later, both she and Eirene were in our bed, jumping up and down, wanting to turn on the lights.

You know your life has turned upside down when you've unpacked two trunks and made scrambled eggs and sausage for everyone before 5:15 am.

We're doing well, I guess. We visited a school yesterday. A lovely place. The fees were higher than Steve's college tuition. I laid in bed that night for two hours, thoughts all over the map. Prayed. Thought about schools. Wondered why I wasn't sleeping. Listened to Steve breathing deeply. Wished I were Steve, but then I remembered - I get insomnia when I'm pregnant.

!!!! We're expecting!!!!!!!!! I guessed we were before we left for Delhi, then confirmed it with a home test before getting on the plane. The baby should come at the end of October. Eirene overheard Steve mention it, and got so excited we thought she'd never stop jumping. She told Isabel immediately, who then turned around, started rubbing my belly and asked, "Is the baby in der?" They're split on their vote. Eirene wants a brother, Isabel, a sister. Does this mean their prayers cancel each other out?

Throughout the trip, we felt God's hand. Steve was wonderful. He pampered his nauseous wife, lovingly and firmly handled his two overcharged children, and managed heavy carry-on bags for 36 hours. God's peace was all over him. I don't mean to insinuate that it was easy. It's never easy; but, it was covered. We felt enveloped in care. God is good, but also, so much more than good. Mere words cannot describe Him.

Our God is truly magnificent. We stand in awe of Him as we look back, and as we move forward. There are issues at the bank that need sorting from when Steve's wallet was stolen six weeks ago. Also, we just learned that a final email didn't get to our supporters. For all they know, we're still in India!

We love you.

For Him,
Robin, for us all

13 March 2004

Hello Dear India Family,

I've been thinking of you often, writing emails in my head.

First, thank You Lord, Eirene is in school. We enrolled her in a small, private school located on the other side of town, but the long drive is good for us. It forces us to get acclimated to city traffic again and meet people. Between my nausea and our culture shock, some days we just want to stay home and ignore the world. Last week, Eirene had a complete meltdown in the Super Walmart. There was just too much stuff and before we knew it, she was crying. The obligation of school is good for us.

My dad's mom passed away last week. We're happy she's finally free from pain, but sad we didn't get to see her one last time. Everyone who had visited her recently said her health had stabilized, that visiting her next month would be fine, but last week, her health plummeted, and then she was gone. I felt cheated. Would have loved to tell her about the baby. The next morning, I was outside early enough to see the sunrise. The colors filled the sky. From one end to the other, the entire sky was pink. It was so beautiful that I lost my breath for a second. Then I thought, *for the first time in her life, my grandma didn't have to wait for the sun to rise. Where she is, the Son never goes down.* I am happy for her.

Between the girls, Isabel asks more frequently than Eirene about going back to India. I didn't anticipate that she would have a harder time adjusting to the move than Eirene, but now it makes sense. In India, Eirene attended preschool, but Isabel was always at home. Her whole world was all of you. Now that we're back here, Eirene is, once again, in school, but Isabel is still home. When we're driving in the car, she asks if we're going to see our friends, and then she names you all, one-by-one. She doesn't forget a single name. We thank God that she's verbal, that she's getting her thoughts out so that we can talk through these things with her, but you can imagine the pull on our heartstrings as we listen. Know that you're in our hearts and prayers.

Grateful we're all in the hands of a loving, merciful God,
Robin, for us all

On Monday, April 26, our India family called to tell us that the son of our nearest American neighbours had been diagnosed with rabies. It was too horrible to comprehend. My nearest neighbour's 9-year-old was going to die of rabies?

India is full of stray dogs. Every now and then during our time in the mountains, word would fly through town that a rabid dog had been spotted. Parents were urged to keep their children indoors until the problem was dealt with. Unfortunately, the locals never seemed to know what to do. There were no officially trained dog catchers, no local pound. Invariably, a group of men armed with large sticks would go off to try to find the animal, but often, even when they found it, they didn't kill it. They didn't know how, and were usually as scared as the rest of us.

Our neighbours had instilled a fear of rabies into their son. He knew that if one of the local strays ever bit him, he was to immediately inform his parents. He loved the strays that roamed the hillside, but he knew that even if he was nicked in fun, he was to inform his parents. The doctors never found a bite mark. The boy had cuts and scrapes from his daily traipsing through the woods, though. Did an infected dog lick one of his scratches? What an unspeakable tragedy to be infected from a loving lick.

We got the call on Monday. By Wednesday, April 28, he was gone. As soon as I heard, I called the missionary hospital. I am notoriously bad at remembering numbers. The fact that I remembered the hospital's phone number was the first miracle. The second one occurred when the doctor himself answered the phone, not one of the nurses. He told me his first-hand account, and then put the mother, my close friend, on the phone. We cried together across the miles. It was horrible.

Since rabies is an infectious disease, the American embassy informed our neighbours that the Indian government would in no way issue a death certificate which could thereby allow them to take their son's body out of the country. They would have to bury him in the Himalayas. The funeral and burial would take place the very next day. No embalming of bodies means burials are required within 24 hours of death.

My neighbour had to hang up rather quickly. It was time for her to have the last viewing of the body before they put her little boy in the casket. Her son had been an energetic 9-year-old boy with a sweet spirit. He'd played with Eirene, even though she was a girl three years younger than he. My neighbour's sweet boy died of rabies - of all ridiculous and horrible things - and here we were in Austin doing what? Re-painting our house? Driving in traffic?

I wanted nothing more than to go back to India where life is hard and real. A few days after our friends buried their son, I wrote this letter to our financial supporters:

1 May 2004

Dear Friends,

We have always tried to be honest about life in India. It was both wonderful and awful. We got sick. We were lonely. We often asked unanswerable questions: Why are people beaten for their faith? Why does anyone have to die of starvation? Why do we Christians waste so much time arguing theology instead of just loving our neighbors? Why were we robbed? This week, we asked "Why did our friends' son have to die?"

A few days ago, our neighbors' youngest son died of rabies. He had felt moderately ill for a while, but his parents never imagined he'd contracted rabies, and he couldn't remember receiving a bite from any of the stray dogs he played with. By the time it was diagnosed, it was too late. For two days, our friends stayed with their son, knowing he was dying and that there was nothing they could do. Oh God, why did our friends have to bury their son? Why do people suffer?

Steve and I are drawn to the book of Job like never before. We see now that it's not a book about suffering. It's a book about faith. At the beginning of the story, Satan states that Job only loves God because God has *put a hedge around him.* He's accusing God of being the type of politician who wins by rigging the election. The two discuss it and decide that Job's response will prove or disprove Satan's challenge. A wealthy man, Job had much to lose. The question was, would he continue to trust God even after losing it all? It's a question that includes us all. Are humans truly free? We have the freedom to descend. Adam and everyone who has ever lived has proven that. But, do we likewise have the freedom and ability to ascend, to believe God for no reason at all? Can a person believe, even when God appears to be the enemy?

Job spends much time in his book ranting and raving. Finally, he is forced to admit that regardless of what he might think, God is not on trial here. Job is. The point of Job's story is not where is God, but where is Job?

Life is unmanageable. Most days, we humans are pretty good at pretending to have everything under control. We smile and say we're fine when anyone asks. We keep our kids busy in after-school activities. We keep ourselves busy, too, and when we're not, we watch TV. However, all the while, we have questions we're afraid to ask, problems we're afraid to admit. What did Steve and I learn in India? We don't want to pretend anymore. We want to be like Job, a man who stated the obvious – "I'm in pain!" – and then refused to budge until God met with him face-to-face, no matter what His answer was.

Will we believe even if, even when? Job did. In the midst of his horror, he said, *This I know; that my Avenger lives, and he, the Last, will take his stand on earth. After my awaking, he will set me close to him, and from my flesh I shall look on God. He whom I shall see will take my part: these eyes will gaze on him and find him not aloof* (Job 19:25-27).

Until that day, Dear Friends, we love you. We love Him.

Steve and Robin

(Some thoughts taken from Philip Yancey's *The Bible Jesus Read*)

13 May 2004

Dear India Family,

Here's a quick glimpse of our lives so you know how much you're missed - Isabel came into my room just now when I was looking at a photo on the computer screen. After she crawled up on my lap (She's all legs these days, is growing so tall.), I pointed out everyone in the photo, then said, "Oh, and Isabel, we also got a message from Mr. R in India!" I clicked on the message and read it aloud.

Isabel said, "I want to see his picture."

Uh-oh. I guess she figured that since the other email included a photo, Mr. R's would, too. When I said there was no picture, she burst into tears and yelled, "I want to see Mr. R! I miss Mr. R!" It was so hard to hear that I hugged her, and so sweet that I had to smile.

I guess the point of all this is that I'm becoming comfortable with the fact that I understand God very little. He's so far outside my box that to think I ever tried to put Him in one makes me laugh. Or cry, as the case may be. During one of our recent debrief sessions, we made a list of the Basic Truths About God that we learned in India. My first one was *I am not God*. Steve took one look at that, laughed aloud and said, "We had to go all the way to India for you to learn THAT?" Ridiculously, not only did I have to go all the way to India to learn it, but had to come all the way home again to say it. I am so slow!

We love and miss you,

Robin, for us all

29 September 2004

Dear Friends and Family,

Have you ever heard the phrase *our faith saw us through*? We've been meditating lately on what it is that's seen us through during these months of readjustment to life in America. Not our own faith, certainly. As we've struggled to reorient ourselves to this land of meticulously kept yards and air conditioning, this land of comfort where pain is avoided at great cost, we've experienced that it is God who is the Faithful One. What has sustained us is His honest dealings with us, His surety of His own work in us, not our own determination to be positive or have faith.

Re-adjustment has also been a joy. What's not to like? We can open our mouths wide while showering. The electricity always stays on. Grandparents live close by. Playgrounds are clean. Swimming lessons are possible, and public libraries are free goldmines. We'd be lying if we said we didn't enjoy the comforts. We don't wax nostalgic about bucket baths, a house so cold that you can see your breath, and sporadically-working phones, though we do miss the forced reliance upon God that those discomforts bring.

We have moved back into our old house. Steve is working at the same firm where he worked before India. Eirene attends school. Isabel helps me around the house while her *didi* (older sister) is at school. Baby Three should make an appearance soon (due date Oct 27). We even drive a mini-van. How long will we live here? Will we return to India? What about another country? We are open. God is faithful, after all. What would we gain by being closed?

Thank you for the patience you have extended during these months. Thank you for your emails, letters and phone calls. We pray God's peace to your families.

Love,
Steve and Robin, Eirene, Isabel and Baby Three

18 November 2004
Dear India Family,

And now, a birth story.

Most of you know that I was 6 cm dilated for 12 days before Aaron was born. You know this because I wrote often, complaining about it. Sorry about that. The first time we went to the birthing center, thinking it was Time, we came home four hours later a little more dilated, a lot more tired, and irrational. Blamed the midwife for not inducing labor like they would have at a normal hospital. Hospital staff would never have allowed me to go home 5 cm dilated, not in this age of litigation. But, no, we have to be different! Steve was very gracious during those days with his depressed, still-pregnant wife. He kept reminding me of the biggest lesson we learned in India: we are not God. God is God, and His timing is perfect. Yes...but...and so 12 days passed. I hibernated at home to avoid the ever-popular greeting, "Wow! You haven't had that baby yet," accompanied by a pat to my belly.

Finally, suddenly, in the early morning hours of October 22, it was all over. Steve put this little baby on my chest, loved on me for a minute or two, and then said, "Hey, what did we have?"

Steve looked, and then, "It's a boy! Robin, you have a son."

"A son? We have a boy? A boy! Well, welcome Aaron Robert."

Aaron is the name of my mother's dad. Robert is my father's father. It is the only boy's name we have ever wanted, but never had reason to use. God has kept a place for this little guy in our hearts for years, ever since I was pregnant with Eirene. Don't get me wrong. We love our girls, and would have been thrilled with another one, but now we know why that name never left our minds. God knew that one day we'd need it. Our Aaron is finally here.

Aaron will be four weeks old tomorrow. We already can't remember life without him.

He was born on October 22. With my birthday on November 22 and Eirene's on December 22, everything fits just right.

Love you all!
Robin, for the Smiths 5

In May of 2005, I wrote to a close friend in India about how we were doing:

We're so grateful for the difficulties we experienced in India. They turned our head knowledge about God into heart knowledge. Before India, we knew a lot about Him, but being swept into India's unmanageable situations finally showed us that head knowledge does not sustain. Our pat answers and limited understanding of tough issues like suffering and predestination, our preconceived notions about God - they all fell flat during those 2 1/2 years. When things got tough, we didn't need to listen to yet another sermon by another famous speaker or read another book. We needed to know in our souls that God was in control. We didn't understand Him. We didn't like what was happening to us or our friends. Was He really in charge, or not? We struggled. We wrestled. We demanded, How could You, our *Loving* God allow us (and/or our friends) to suffer? We still don't know the answer to the question. We do know that God is good. In fact, He is the actual definition of goodness.

I can hear your voice in my head, "OK, what's next?" I'm glad you asked! Our home church here in Austin is reinstating an old, almost-forgotten vision to see churches planted in Turkey. A group of us will embark on a scouting trip in August. We Smiths are busy applying for new passports, including one for Aaron. I can't believe I'm saying this, but it seems the India chapter of the Grand Adventure to which God has called us is completed.

The India chapter...is completed. Those words make me laugh now, but I believed them when I wrote them.

When we moved to India in 2001, we didn't exactly have hearts for the lost. We didn't see ourselves as evangelists or pastors. All we knew for sure was that we wanted to be overseas, to do something, to be used by God. The organization we joined gave us the chance to do that. Steve used his engineering skills. I helped mentor the interns. We both ran the house. Designing hospitals, orphanages and schools was satisfying, for a time. Somewhere along the way, though, we began to wonder about the effectiveness of the work. One day, I was looking over Steve's shoulder at yet another set of plans for yet another orphanage. He was editing the plans (or whatever it is that civil engineers do), and all of a sudden I voiced the question that had been in my mind for weeks, "How many more orphanages do we need to design for India to be reached?" Steve looked at me, then silently nodded his head. I think it was in that moment that we knew we were not long for that type of work.

If it's true, as the church in South India claims, that the apostle Thomas was martyred in India, then the gospel has been in India as long as it's been anywhere, yet today India is still considered an unreached nation. Christian schools, hospitals and orphanages abound, but have yet to make a significant impact with the gospel. How can that be? How is it that Hindu parents fight to get their children admitted into Christian schools for the good education, but are not changed by the Message their children hear? The same is true for orphanages and hospitals. During our time in India, we saw a lot of Christian busyness, but we never heard of anyone bearing much Fruit.

We didn't have the courage to voice our questions or doubts about service projects during our 2 1/2 years in the mountains, but once we got back to the States, we began to honestly consider the problem of busyness-but-no-disciples. Thus, when our church asked us to consider joining them in the renewed work in Turkey, we were excited. They were asking the same questions about fruit and effectiveness. We now cared more about the unreached and their need to hear His Name than our personal skills or training, what we thought we were good at or comfortable with. This was a radical shift in our perspective about missions. We'd spent over two years "doing something" for God in north India. Now, we were asking: "What is God doing, and how can we join Him in it?"

We visited Turkey with high hopes. Everyone said that after living in India for 2+ years, we'd find Turkey pretty easy, and they were right. Compared to where we'd been, Turkey was clean, beautiful and organized. Modern. And only half as far away from the grandparents as India! The people were polite. Helpful. The girls were thrilled to be traveling again. Aaron gave us no trouble. However, lovely as it was, our hearts were closed. No excitement. No desire. We were shocked. How could we not want to live in this beautiful place? Nothing felt right. The food was bland (more chutney needed!). They made chai without milk or cardamom (who does that?). There weren't even any monkeys (how boring)! We came back home willing to move to Turkey long-term, but hoping that God would help us *want* to go.

A month after our return, Steve and I went out for a date one night. At some point during the meal, one of us finally admitted to missing India. Whoever said it first - to this day, I cannot remember who - spoke with trepidation, convinced the other would walk out of the restaurant without a backward glance. Wonder of wonders, as soon as the words were spoken, the other of us agreed, and that was it. We began to pray for God to take us back to India.

The question was, where should we go? How to serve? We knew that, due to the great need in India, we could call any of the ministries we'd served during our 2 1/2 years, state our desire to help, and they'd ask how soon we could buy the tickets. "Warm body? Willing to help? Come on over!" We wanted more than that. We knew that wherever we served, life would be hard. We had no romantic notions the second time around. The last thing we wanted was to generate something on our own efforts. We didn't just want God to make the phone call. We *needed* Him to. We prayed, "God, would You send someone to us? Don't let us make something happen. Would You make the phone call?"

A couple of weeks passed. We felt rudderless. One morning, Steve said he was going to spend the day fasting about India. We don't fast very often. I am weak. In my flesh, I'd probably rather do anything than fast. Yet, as soon as Steve said he was going to fast, I got excited that, with Aaron weaned, I could join him in it! That had to be God. Steve left for work. I started my day. I got so lost in my routine with the kids and housework that at one point I forgot I was fasting and went into the kitchen to make a snack. Opened the cupboard, then remembered I wasn't eating. I share this to show that my fast that day was anything but "holy." There were no long periods of quiet Bible study or wonderfully long conversations with God about our future. Mostly, it was laundry and diapers. When I remembered to pray, it was quick one-liners, "Please, God, make the phone call."

Midmorning, the phone rang. A friend of ours from India was currently in the States. She and her husband had been thinking about us for a long time. Even though we had visited Turkey a short time ago, would we consider moving back to India to work with them?

We talked for about 45 minutes. I smiled through the entire conversation. I couldn't believe it. God had literally made the phone ring! The humans had been theorizing, God acting practically.

As soon as we finished our conversation, I called Steve at his office, "Is this a good time to talk? Are you sitting down?"

Steve felt the energy through the line. He heard it in my voice. He said, "You're about to ruin my life, aren't you?"

"Yes," I blurted, and then told him the whole story. Then, silence for us both. There was nothing to say. Our lives had just changed forever, again.

A new city - Delhi. 20 million people. Down there in the plains that had so terrified me when we lived in the mountains. A completely different type of work than we'd ever done before. Would it be an easier season or harder? Would the girls be happy to return? How would Aaron adapt to India? So many questions. The only answer we had was the ultimate one - Jesus. He Himself would be the Answer to every question we could ever ask.

Not to us, O Lord, not to us, but to Your Name goes all the glory
for Your unfailing love and faithfulness.
Our God is in the heavens...He does as He wishes.
Their idols are merely things of silver and gold, shaped by human hands.
They have mouths but cannot talk, and eyes but cannot see.
They have ears but cannot hear, and noses but cannot smell.
They have hands but cannot feel, and feet but cannot walk,
and throats but cannot make a sound.
O Israel, trust the LORD!
He is your helper; He is your shield.
(Psalm 115)

January 2007 - October 2011

More Pruning

No half measures will do.
[Not] to only prune a branch here
and a branch there...
[He] wants the whole tree out!
(C.S. Lewis, *Mere Christianity*)

To be sensitive to the people with whom we worked from 2007-2011, I have purposefully kept certain details about this season of our lives vague.

28 January 2007

Dear Dad,

It's so nice having Mom with us to help us get settled. Thanks for sharing her. A month is a long time to be apart. Having one adult per child on this trip made a world of difference. Even navigating the Delhi airport with our 19 suitcases and trunks was easy. Well, if not easy, it definitely was not the nightmare it could have been. The final hurdle was hauling those 19 pieces of luggage up to our temporary housing - a third-floor walk-up.

We made a decision on a permanent place last night. It's a newly built, private home. The landlord and her family occupy the first two floors. We will live on the top floor, a separate apartment. The owners have a daughter who is a little older than Eirene. Perhaps we'll even get a friend out of the bargain.

It's a huge apartment. Maybe about 2000 sq. ft? At first I was embarrassed to consider it, but then realised that the extra space will make hosting guests that much easier. The location is great, too. Steve can walk to the office.

Meanwhile, living in this current apartment feels like camping. There is no dining table, we eat our meals on the floor. Thankfully, a new store is nearby, so staples are easy to find. The store manager already knows Aaron by name, and even took a photo of him with his phone. He gives the children free candy every time we shop, while I practice my Hindi with the workers. They have kindly remarked several times that my Hindi is good. I don't have the heart to tell them that food and grocery items comprise 90% of my vocabulary. Maybe I can mention 8 or 9 different kinds of lentils by name, but don't ask me if it's raining outside!

The new store does not stock produce, unfortunately. We must buy fruits and vegetables from the sellers who push their carts past our apartment building every morning. Sitting in our living room up here on the third floor, we can hear them yelling about their products. They're not the only ones shouting, though.

First are the men riding bicycles, the recycling guys. Supposedly, they buy people's recyclable items, but so far we've been out of luck. It's hard to run down these three flights of stairs fast enough to catch them before they ride away, but also, we simply don't understand the system. One day, Steve stood down on the street, determined to catch them before they could get away, but he couldn't get anyone to buy our pile. At one point, one of the recycling guys came over to see what Steve had, but as soon as he looked at Steve's pile, he shook his head as if in disbelief, jumped back on his bicycle, and rode off with the all the others. We hope to figure out the system before too much piles up again.

After the recycling guys, the trash collectors come yelling down the street. Then come the vegetable and fruit guys. We can't understand a word of what they shout as they walk. I wonder if this is how non-native English speakers feel about hot dog vendors at baseball games? We finally decided to just run and look over the balcony at every yell or shout. When it turns out to be a fruit or vegetable seller, off I go, down the stairs to catch him before he leaves. And then the dance begins. IF he is there, and has the produce I want, I ask the price. Some bargain with me. Some refuse. If they refuse, then I go back up and wait for the next one.

So, there you have it - week one. Grocery shopping in Delhi. Oh, and, in case you missed it, we're having a ball. It's great to be back! Thanks for your prayers.

Love,
Robin, for us all (and Mom, too!)

31 August 2007
Dear Mom and Dad,

Four months ago, we said goodbye to our co-workers for the summer, experienced Delhi's blistering heat for the first time, and wondered how in the world we were going to fill the scorching months ahead. Tonight, I write to tell you that God is faithful. He will not (in no way, never) call us to something that He will not also give us the grace to endure. Hallelujah! Back in May, Steve and I started to pray the same, very simple prayer everyday, "Lord, let us do more than just 'survive' the heat." He took that prayer and ran with it! It was a great summer.

Our visa-run to Thailand was the holiday we didn't know we needed. It was so refreshing that we stayed two extra days. Back here at home, frequent guests kept us entertained. So far, God has taken us "at our word" and kept the guest room full. We love it.

We also made some changes at the office - painted, rearranged, sorted and tossed. Steve introduced a new Bible study approach to the staff, and Aaron learned he absolutely loves taking coconut for communion. The staff are good to him, giving him as many of the left-over pieces as he can hold in his hand, and then some!

We spent two weeks back in our old "stomping grounds" up in the mountains. Studied Hindi everyday (including the kids), and enjoyed every minute hiking around and visiting with old friends. Even so, we all agreed it was good to come back home to Delhi. Our memories of that place are precious, but we are grateful to be here, doing what God has called us to now. This place that used to terrify me is now my home.

Our co-workers will return from the States in a couple of weeks. We anticipate several days of discussion and prayer with them about what God might want to do in the coming months. There are many things we could do, but we want the Lord to show us which ones are on His agenda and which are not. Our constant prayer is to stay open to His leading, that we don't become enamored with our own agenda and lose sight of His, especially the main one, that His Son will be worshiped by people from every tribe, nation and tongue. He is worth it!

Much love,
Robin, with Steve, Eirene, Isabel and Aaron

1 November 2007
Dear Mom and Dad,

We're doing well. Weather here is absolutely gorgeous. Reaches the low 90s F in the afternoon, but it's so dry in Delhi this time of year, that it cools off at night. We haven't slept with AC since September. I didn't know that Delhi would have comfortable temperatures. Nor did I understand about the dirt. This stuff isn't dust. I'm talking Dirt. Consider the guest room. It has no windows. Not a single one. When the power goes out, it's pitch black in there. Even so, we must dust that room daily. When we don't, dirt piles up on the floor. Little piles of it, as if someone were potting plants in there. There is just that much dirt in the air. I thought the trees out front were dying, but no, the leaves are just covered with dirt. Brush it away and you see green. We mop the floors daily, but still have to wash the kids' feet before bed each night. Even if they spend the entire day inside this apartment, the bottoms of their feet are black with dirt!

No complaints, though. We're relieved to be done with July's high humidity+105F temps. Kids are doing well. Aaron turned three last month. He loves sitting on his stool in the school area with us, "reading" his books while the girls do their work. He also likes starting the timer and saying, "Ready, steady, GO" for the timed tests in math.

There are lots of guests these days, too. Hosting is a gracious gift of fellowship that God brings right to our door. Since February, we've had 57 overnight guests! Isn't that great? God is answering our prayer to fill this giant apartment.

Better go. Time for Aaron to take a nap, and for the girls and me to get back to work.

Love you much,
Robin, for us all

30 November 2007

Dear Mom and Dad,

What an eventful month! Where do I even begin?

It all started with the Festival of Lights, Diwali, the largest Hindu festival of the year. People decorate their houses and give gifts. Commercials on TV advertise Diwali sales. It's as big for them as Christmas is for us. Sadly, while Christmas celebrates the Light that's already come, Diwali is meant to entice the Light. Hindus clean and decorate their homes, and light candles and lamps hoping that the goddess of fortune will be attracted to the light, enter their homes, and bring fortune with her. The holiday is ripe for redemption, though. Christ is the Light of the world. He didn't need to be enticed, but came purposefully, and He loves to give good gifts to His children. We need to pray about how to celebrate Him as the True Light of Diwali in years to come, but we weren't quite ready to tackle it this year. Instead, my birthday became the excuse we needed to have our neighbours over for a *satsung* (worship service) and introduce them to the God we worship. We pushed the living room furniture back to the walls and covered the floor with rugs. Everyone took their shoes off at the door, and sat cross-legged on the floor. We lit a candle, and used half of a coconut shell as the candlestick. Candles and coconuts are considered holy to most Hindus. By incorporating these items into the service, we signaled to our neighbors that this was a holy place and time. Giving the elements a "Jesus" twist is easy. The candle reminds us that Jesus is the True Light of the World. The broken coconut shell symbolizes His Body, the Ultimate Sacrifice.

The man who led the service also sat on the floor. He wore a saffron colored scarf around his neck. Saffron is considered a holy color and the scarf signified that he was the leader of the service, like a pastor's robes or collar in the West. He laid his Bible on a small, wooden pedestal (important to keep it off the ground), while the musicians sat on the floor next to him playing traditional instruments. After we all sang some Hindi songs, the leader shared from the Word. He spoke from his heart - caste is bad, Jesus is the Answer for India, let us treat others as we want to be treated. It was the same kind of message we'd hear at a service back in Texas - Jesus is the Answer, and we're called to love our neighbor. Finally, we took communion with coconut. The coconut fruit was the bread; the milk was the wine.

Our neighbours loved it. They stayed for hours, eating and talking about the peace they felt, and how encouraged they were. It was an absolutely wonderful evening. God was lifted up in our house by our neighbors. Who could have known that before the end of our first year here, our Sikh neighbors would sing praises to Jesus in our living room? Several days later, one of our neighbors was still talking about it, how she'd never felt peace like that. "Jesus' peace," she called it. Oh, Lord, may there be many more chances!

Later, during Thanksgiving week, the ministry hosted its third annual foot-washing event. Sixty-five Americans came to Delhi to wash the feet of low caste and Dalits. Foot-washing? Let me explain.

In the West, we have few taboos concerning feet and shoes. "No shoes, no shirt, no service," is about it for us. We even wear shoes *inside* our houses, for goodness' sake! Here in the East, shoes and feet are considered unholy, impure things. People remove their shoes for auspicious events, and never put their feet on a piece of furniture.

Not only are feet in India unclean, but people can be, too. High caste people become unclean if they touch persons of low caste. Some of our high caste neighbors have servants who have worked for them for years, but our neighbors never call their servants by name. They call the guard, "Guard," and the washing girl, "Washing Girl." It's surreal to be surrounded by people who aren't called their names or touched. Can you imagine? Jesus could. First century Palestine had much in common with today's India. At foot-washing events, we touch low caste people. On purpose. Without fear. Not just their heads or hands. We touch their feet. This was the third annual Thanksgiving foot-washing. It was wonderful.

In one village, a community leader spoke to the crowd after watching a few people get their feet washed. He is Sikh. In his religion, people do penance for sin by washing shoes or feet. Yet, here we were, a whole group of people who'd done nothing wrong, washing the feet of his fellow villagers. He declared that Jesus must be the Answer for his country!

After three days of foot-washings, and then stuffing ourselves with Thanksgiving goodies, we headed off for our final event of the month - a wedding of close friends from our mountain days. Steve drove defensively for 8 hours over 170 miles of Indian roads. We celebrated the joining of two hearts, spent a few restful days in the (cold!) mountains, and are now home again. Being tired but not tired out is an amazing feeling.

Thanks for letting me take you on this whirlwind tour of November!

We love you,
Robin and all

In July of 2008, we enrolled Eirene in a local, Indian school. Eventually, all our children would become students there, but Eirene was the trailblazer, not only for our family, but also for the school. She was the first western student they had ever enrolled. Of the 1200 students in grades 1-12, our little fourth grader was the only blonde, the only native English speaker.

The following is an email I wrote to friends, career missionaries who had "been there and done that" on the Field:

5 August 2008
Dear K and W,

I'm so glad God laid Eirene on your heart. This transition to school has gone better than we could have imagined, but it's still hard. For one thing, all the children miss my parents. Saying goodbye after seeing them in Norway in July was hard, so hard in fact - even for me-that I still can't talk about it. So, there's that. Also, deep down, the kids would rather live in Austin than here. Yes, things are going well here, and yes, we all know that God has called us here. Even so, the kids would rather be home (in Austin), so if it's a hard day at school, it's easy for Eirene to slip into I-miss-Gramma-and-Grampa mode. Emotions spiral down from there.

So far, the school seems to be a good fit. Her classmates all want to be her friend. The teachers were so impressed with her poise that they signed her up for the debate club. Her first debate will be tomorrow, an inter-school debate on the traffic problems here in Delhi.

Not only will she need to give the speech into a microphone with voice inflection and hand motions, but when she's done, the judges might actually question her about some of her points. She's nervous. This morning she didn't want to go to school, but kept crying about missing my parents.

God is doing deep things in her heart through all of this. She's learning to trust Him. Truthfully, we're all learning to trust Him. We cherish your prayers!

Blessings to you both,
Robin and All

29 September 2008
Dear Mom and Dad,

The other day, our house helper, Meenu, rushed through the front door, bag of newly purchased veggies in her hand, apologizing for her late return, but also excited to tell us why. The landlady's guard had wanted to talk. He'd noticed she'd missed a week of work. How was it that she still had a job?

"It was really OK with your boss that you were gone for so long?" the guard asked.

"Yes. They understood that I was sick and needed to stay home."

"Why are they so good to you?"

"Because they worship a good God. Your boss (our landlord) doesn't worship good gods. Your boss doesn't know how to love. My bosses know how to love because their God is good."

"Oh, you mean that *foreign* god that they worship."

Apparently, after hearing that remark, Meenu spent several minutes informing the guard how the Only God Who Is can't be foreign. He just is who He is. She said that if he would attend satsung with us on Sunday afternoons, he would be able to hear more about the One God. The Truth would expand his mind and make his life better. The guard said that Meenu spoke good words, but that he would never get permission to attend satsung. Later that day, one of the office staff followed up with the guard. If he's not able to attend satsung, we will make sure that guys from the office come here to speak with him.

Amazing! We've been praying for our landlady's family since we moved into this house. Even Isabel and Eirene pray for chances to speak with her daughter about the Jesus. How could we have known that giving Meenu time off when she was sick would speak so loudly?

95

To paraphrase a famous saying, truly, they know we are different by our love.

I haven't told you very much about Meenu. I don't know what I'd do without her. She began working for us two months after we moved in. As you can tell from this story, she has a deep faith.

Meenu's life is hard. Her parents are dead. She left her husband because he is a drunk who used to beat her and the kids. She can't afford to feed and care for both of her sons, so the younger one lives with her sister. She travels for two hours by bus to get to our house by 10:00 each morning. Traveling by bus in Delhi is not pretty. Most passengers are men. They verbally harass her. It is standing room only. There is no AC. Pickpockets abound. Just getting here is a struggle, and then she has to start work!

Being single in this male dominated society isn't easy. Judges in divorce court pay her no mind because there is no male to represent her case. Potential landlords ignore her because her husband doesn't live with her, and everybody *knows* that single women are loose. In the middle of all this hardship, we catch Meenu praying as she washes dishes. We hear her singing as she sweeps the floors. She loves our children as if they were her own.

Sometimes I wonder if following Jesus makes a difference in people's lives, but Meenu says that following Jesus is the best decision she ever made. God is the Father she lost, the Mother she misses, the Husband who will never beat her, the Dad who cares for her boys, the Judge who never takes a bribe, and the Shelter she needs when landlords think the worst of her. Meenu told the guard what she knows from experience - there is no foreign god. There is only One God, He is good, and He is the only hope for her nation. Meenu loves her country, but she knows it is not a good place. She longs for change, but knows it will only occur when people begin to worship the Good God, the God worthy of respect, the Only God powerful enough to change people for the better.

Meenu often says that we changed her life. The truth is, she blesses us. Please pray for Meenu and her sons today, and for the millions of other Meenus here in the subcontinent.

All my love,
Robin (and all)

9 January 2009
Dear Mom and Dad,

It seems that our landlady wants us to move. She called Steve on Monday to ask if we'd let her show the flat to a new family. What? !! When we met with her before Christmas, we thought that we'd all agreed to extend our lease until after our trip to America in April. Can someone say, *communication gap*?

We're not stressed, but we are asking the Lord to be clear. He always is when we give Him time to be. Please pray for us sheep as we wait for instructions from the Gentle Shepherd.

Love,
Robin, for us all

5 February 2009
Dear Mom and Dad,

On January 9th, I wrote asking for prayer. On the 12th, we signed a lease on our new, better apartment! Talk about clear direction! We now live on a dead-end street that's not only quieter and safer for the kids, but closer to the office for Steve. A young doctor and his family live on the ground floor. We live on the middle floor, but the top floor is ours, too. We'll make it a true guest suite, complete with kitchen, sitting area, bedroom, and a large terrace (play space for the kids). In terms of square footage, this new place is smaller than the old one, but we're glad. Smaller and more intimate setting, but still room for guests? God answers prayer more fully than we can imagine!

Do you remember the last move you made? If I remember correctly, you packed boxes, rented a truck, and paid us in pizza for helping. Our move was not that. No truck. Lots of people. Lots of tea. Lots of rope.

How do you move in India? First, you hire a guy with a bicycle-powered cart. He brings his friends. They load as much as they can in the cart while you fill your own car with as much as you can. Then, you drive or walk to the new house. You unload. Big things that won't fit up the stairwell, you hoist up and over the balcony with five men and a rope. You yell, "No, that won't work" a lot. You find stools for the men to stand on as they push items up and over the balcony while you pull on the rope from above. You cringe as you watch your bed being hoisted up and over the balcony, hoping it (or the house) doesn't get too banged up. You forgive them for breaking the glass on the side table. You make and serve chai a...g...a...i...n. And, at the end of the day, as you pay them, you remember that they did all of that for $4.00 each, and that your neighbours would never pay them that much. You remember that these men are so poor that when you served them water, they told you to just pour the water into their cupped hands, and they lapped it up instead of using cups. You realise that your new, downsized apartment is bigger than anything they've seen in their lives. Finally, you recognize that these men - the dirty, smelly, poorest-of-the-poor on the planet - are dearly loved by the God who made them, that they are made in His image, and while you're consumed with thoughts about all the clean-up you'll have to do once they leave, He's loving them unto death, even death on a cross. Your sleep is a humbled one that night, and you joyfully hire them the next day to finish the job.

Love you madly,
Robin and all

15 April 2009

Dear Friends and Family,

Greetings from Austin! We have several reasons to visit this summer. First, we miss you, our friends and family, and want to reconnect. We also want to share about what the Lord has done in the ministry and our own lives over the past 2.5 years. Finally, we need some rest. We are physically and emotionally tired, though not discouraged.

God called us as a family to live in India. Below are some reasons why...

- One-third of the world's poor are Indian.
- Almost half of India's population (43%) is illiterate.
- In the UN Development Indices of education, sanitation/ health, and economic development, India rates lower than every sub-Saharan African nation.
- 80% of Indians live on less than $2.00 per day.
- The most heartbreaking point of all - India is home to 72% of the world's UPGs (Unreached People Groups*).

We pray that your hearts become more drawn to the place we call home. We look forward to seeing you all soon!

Love,
Steve, for all
(*A UPG is a group of people with their own language and culture in which, if there are Christians at all, they are so few in number and/or

resources that they are unable to influence their own people for Christ. The only hope a UPG has to hear about Christ is from an outsider.)

28 June 2009
Dear Friends and Family,

All too quickly, our time in America has come to an end. Tomorrow, we Smiths begin the long journey home. This visit has been rich. We're so grateful that we came, but also glad to return to routine, our own beds (!), and good Indian food.

We recently read that centuries ago, *Celtic missionaries sailed in boats without sails or rudders so that God might let His tides and storms move them to whatever shore He wished them to go...the cry of the voyager was never for better weather, but only that the boat should remain intact 'til God, who kept them afloat, should land them where He wished them to serve their world.**

Our God hasn't changed. He is still in the business of guiding His children over oceans to whatever shore He wishes. Thank you for helping to make our voyage possible. We covet your prayers as we return to our land of service, and we look forward to the day when all of our "boats" finally land on That Distant Shore!

Love,
Steve and Robin, with Eirene, Isabel and Aaron
(**Celtic Devotions: A Guide to Morning and Evening Prayer*, Calvin Miller)

29 July 2009
Dear Mom and Dad,

It is taking us longer to re-adjust than we thought it would. The crowds, the power outages, the dirt, the humid heat, the constant repairs required just to maintain the house. It all hit us upon our return, and for the first time in a long time, we felt like foreigners.

The other day, I was driving the girls from school to one of their various functions, like almost every other American mom, but then I began to count the differences. For one, I was driving on the other side of the road in a city of 20+million people that sees thousands of new vehicles added to the streets every month. Also, driving these roads feels a bit like playing the old video game Frogger. There are so many things to dodge that I rarely, if ever, shift higher than third gear. There are jay-walkers to avoid, of course, but there are also people living on the street. Literally. Driving to school includes avoiding people doing laundry. I dodge cows, dogs, bullock carts, buses, motorcycles, 3-wheeled vehicles, cars, scooters, bicycles, men pushing carts, trucks, even the occasional elephant, horse and camel. Just your typical suburban housewife, driving her kids to school.

The population continues to astound. There are, literally, millions of people in India who have never heard about Jesus.

Love you much,
Robin and all

27 August 2009
Dear Mom and Dad,

Most Fridays, we facilitate a Bible study in the office. Whoever happens to be in the office at that time is invited. Many different types of people join us.

Last Friday, some men arrived about 15 minutes after we started. We'd never seen them before. They sat down quietly in chairs near the door, on the opposite side of the room, and then listened for the entire hour, contributing a couple of thoughts only near the end of the time.

Currently, we are studying the book of James. Much of the book concerns trials - how to view them, how to navigate them, how God can help us through them. That God can help us through trials isn't a common thought in India. For example, in today's newspaper, there was a photo of several holy men sitting in tubs of water. Their bodies were submerged. Only their heads could be seen, sticking up out of the water. The caption explained it: The holy men (brahman priests) had sat/stood in those tubs of water for four hours, praying for rain. Their hope was that if they stayed in the cold water long enough, the rain gods would pay attention and send rain.

In other words, there is little-to-no understanding among Hindu Indians that God cares about us personally, takes an interest in us, or helps us through trials. The best we can hope for is to somehow catch the god's attention (when the god/gods happen to be awake), and then hope he/she/they are in a request-granting mood.

During last week's Bible study, we talked about how God wants to (and can) help us through trials, then Steve and I encouraged each person to silently give his or her personal trials to God and ask Him to help. After the prayer, one of the men sitting near the door spoke. He had a trial. Could he discuss it with us? He had suffered from a stomach ailment for ten years. He'd seen countless doctors. Spent all his money looking for a cure. Nothing helped. Ten years of pain. Could God help him?

We opened our Bibles and read the story of Jesus healing the woman who had been sick for twelve years. She also had spent all her money on doctors who promised the world, but didn't deliver. We can only imagine how much money our new friend spent over the years, or the crazy prescriptions he received. We once heard of a doctor who claimed he could cure people of HIV by giving them transfusions of clean blood once a month (at a very high price, of course), so anything is possible. Not to mention the fact that, according to karma, if people are sick, it is their fault. They must have done something wrong, either in this life or a previous one, to earn the "curse" of sickness. In the Bible story, Jesus not only didn't berate the woman for being sick, but postponed His visit to the home of a VIP (an important detail in this class-based society), to heal her, a mere woman.

Our new friend listened with wide eyes. We asked if we could pray for him. He nodded, and we did. No grand formula. No loud chanting. Just a simple request - would Jesus heal our new friend the way He'd healed the woman in the story? After the prayer, he asked us to remove the red thread that was tied around his big toe. He'd worn it for years, thinking it was a talisman that would protect him from bad luck. He now knew the thread was powerless.

Later that night, our new friend called the office. He was so sorry if he woke anyone, but he just had to share his news. The pain in his stomach was gone! For the first time in ten years, he was lying down to sleep without pain. Could he come back to talk with us some more about Jesus on another day? Of course!

Rejoicing in our God who loves to heal and save,
Robin and all

30 September 2009

Dear Mom and Dad,

I am really enjoying this Friday study through James. Funny. I avoided the book for years. I could only hear condemnation in his description of true religion. It seemed better to simply leave the book alone.

Then, after Aaron was born, I found myself back in James quite by accident but this time, I found life and hope in the words penned by the man who was Jesus' half-brother. Studying the book again this year here in the Indian context, has made it even more captivating.

In India, because it's a caste based (class based) society, status here is ascribed, not achieved. One's lineage means all. In ascribed status societies, a new-born prince is more valuable than any peasant. Conversely, we Americans believe status can be achieved or attained. We celebrate Abe Lincoln stories. That one of our favourite presidents was born in a log cabin to poor farmers is not something we shamefully hide, but celebrate.

What does this have to do with James? If there was ever a person who could have claimed the right to ascribed status, it was James. He was Jesus' blood relative. In ascribed status societies, everything is about who you are or who you know. Do you want a driver's license, or a good price on your electricity bill? A good school option for your kids? Then, who do you know? Or, who do you know who knows somebody else?

What about James? Did he lay claim to ascribed status? Did he name drop? In the very first verse, he wrote, *James, a servant of God and of the Lord Jesus Christ*. He didn't mention being Jesus' brother. He referred to himself as a servant. I never paid much attention to that verse before. Why would I? I had never experienced the oppression of living in an ascribed status society. I had no eyes to see the true humility of James' introduction, but the people with whom we study on Fridays noticed his choice of words immediately. They were stunned into silence as they tried to contemplate a man who, not only avoided using personal association for gain, but went so far as to introduce himself as a slave, the lowest of the low, a person with no status at all.

We love what we do here, and we love you, too.
Robin and all

29 October 2009

Dear Mom and Dad,

All the kids are in school. It is a new season. Mornings are full. First, the girls. Get breakfast on the table. Make lunches. Fill water bottles. Fix hair according to school regulations. At 7:30, Steve drives them to school. Then, it's Aaron's turn. Clothes, breakfast, snack into his little backpack, driving away by 9:00. Aaron's school is just right for little ones. There are educational games on all the shelves, blocks, books, little chairs, a playground across the street. He does a craft each day. They have snack time. He loves to count - 8 students and 3 adults! He loves school.

Yesterday, Steve visited a different school. There were about 20 students. No chairs. Actually, there was no floor. No books, no pencils, no worksheets, no play-dough, no puzzles. No midmorning snack. Forget playground. They wish they had walls.

This world is full of disparity. Most days, we don't think about it. We go through our days under the illusion that the rest of the world lives pretty much like we do. Sometimes, we even think we're suffering because we don't have what those rich people in magazines have.

We recently learned that there are *illegals* in India. Not illegal aliens. Illegal Indians. Their ancestors were nomadic tribal people. Being landless made it difficult for the British rulers to classify them. At some point, they were declared illegal, a status which has never changed. In their own country. They cannot qualify for registration cards (kind of like our Social Security Numbers). Unregistered people don't exist (technically). Thus, their children aren't allowed in school. The men can't get jobs. The illiteracy rate for these nomadic communities is about 98%. No one knows how many illegals there are, but those who study the problem say that they definitely number in the millions.

A small community of about 150 of these nomadic people live in a tent community on the outskirts of Delhi. One of the office staff has recently started a school for the children in that community. Steve accompanied him on his visit yesterday. We have to tread lightly, though. A week ago, visitors from America toured the school. After they left, a rumor began that they had brought gifts, but the school staff hoarded them all. By the time Steve arrived yesterday, the rumor had grown from simple gifts to $700!

For now, we will concentrate on training the man who started the school and the two teachers he hired. It's interesting, to say the least, helping them think through their lessons. How does a teacher teach without paper, pencils, worksheets, crayons, textbooks, or any basic teaching resources? Forget computers. We're making lesson plans with sticks, dirt, rocks, slates and pieces of chalk.

The needs are overwhelming. Today, a young girl in the community died. She was injured a few months ago, but the family couldn't find a hospital that would help her. It was a simple wound, but it needed professional medical attention. Without it, infection set in. She stopped eating. Today, they buried her.

Psalms 123-124 give great comfort. India's nomadic tribals have had *their fill of contempt*, but God is on their side! Please pray with us that they will learn to *lift their eyes* to Him.

Love you much,
Robin and all

30 November 2009

Dear Mom and Dad,

Last night, a friend of ours told us a story about something that happened in his village when he was in the 7th grade. He even wrote a song about it.

The people in his village worship Kali, the goddess of death. On particular days, devotees bring offerings to the local temple. On one such day, one of the mothers instructed her son to take their offering to the temple.

The boy set out with the traditional offering of homemade chapattis (whole wheat tortillas) and water. He carried the chapattis in a basket on his head, the jug of water in his hand. The boy was about halfway to the temple when he realized he had to go to the bathroom. What to do? Only what all men do in this country when the need strikes them. He looked for the nearest wall, or tree, or rock, then (oops!), dropped two of the chapattis onto the ground and accidentally peed right onto them. It's not easy going to the bathroom while holding a jug of water and balancing a basket on your head. Now what was he supposed to do? The chapattis were no longer good for the offering, but should he just leave them there? What a waste! What choice was there? In the end, he continued to the temple and presented the remaining chapattis to the priest. The priest poured the water over the chapattis in offering to the deity, and the boy, relieved of his obligation to the goddess, set off for home.

Along the way, he passed the spot where he'd dropped the two chapattis, except now, there was a huge pile of wet chapattis. Apparently, as others from the village walked the same path to the temple with their offerings, they saw the boy's chapattis on the ground, covered in what they thought was water. They figured this must also be a holy place, and so person after person left offerings of chapattis covered with water on that spot. So many people were now talking about this new holy site that when the boy arrived home, his mother stopped him with a question - Had he been sure to leave a small offering of chapatis and water at the new holy site, or had he taken the entire offering to the main temple?

Sound too good to be true? Our friend was that little boy. He told us that he had not known what to say to his mother. Would she be angry? In the end, he told her everything. Far from being angry, she told their friends and neighbors the truth about the *holy* site. Eventually, our friend wrote a song about it.

It's funny. And heartbreaking. The villagers mistook a toilet place for a holy place. Nobody asked. Nobody wondered. Rather, these poor, hungry people blindly, desperately sought to appease the goddess of death by laying their homemade bread and precious water on a dirt road where a little boy had gone to the bathroom.

Your speechless daughter,
Robin, for us all

21 January 2010

Hey Mom and Dad,

Thanks so very much for praying for the Leadership Development event. From the first moment, Steve and I were clear about the ground rules - this was a casteless place, everyone was to take turns sharing thoughts and ideas, and none of us were experts. We were all there to learn, and we'd use discussion to do it.

We sat on the floor, gave each person a whole Bible, then read and discussed Psalm 139. Steve and I didn't lecture. We asked questions, and watched where things went.

Our hope was that by the end of the event, people would feel closer to God and closer to each other. Both things happened. We asked for their feedback at the end of Day 2. So far, what the comments have been positive:

- "We should make this mandatory for everyone to attend monthly!"
- "Please next time allow us to invite our wives."
- "You should write up a little synopsis of the time and teachings/lessons learned through these discussions, and give them to us so we can take the information back to our people and share it with them."
- "You should come teach my people now!"

Steve didn't quite know how to reply to that last comment. He said something about how we are westerners and were raised in the western church, so we're hesitant to interact too much with his people. We don't want to turn them into western Christians. The man replied, "No! Do not worry about that! What you know, my people need to know. Who else is there to teach them, unless you come and share with us your knowledge?"

His response shocked us. Steve and I have spent much time and energy avoiding the whole discipleship topic. We don't want to turn Indian followers of Jesus into western Christians. We don't want to be too church-y, or say things out of their cultural context. Yet, here was this man saying, "Stop worrying about it and come!" We can't stop thinking about it.

We know that no matter how long we live here, we will always be considered foreigners. We'll also never know enough to express the Message in cultural ways like the head of this ministry does. However, for the first time we're wondering if perhaps God might lead us to work that we can do? We love discussing our way through the Word with people. The office staff think since the head of the ministry out of the country these days, the work will stop. Maybe they're wrong? What if the work doesn't cease, but instead shifts to include more events like this?

In summary, it was a good event. And exhausting. Listening intently to Hindi then checking for meaning with the translator, trying to keep strong personalities from dominating the discussions, praying continually for humble hearts, juggling the driving duties. I loved every minute of it. We're also grateful to know where people really stand, spiritually. Without this event, we wouldn't know...

- "Women are more important than men." One of the ladies said this not once, but several times. I finally told her it wasn't true. Women are not more important than men, and men are not more important than women. She was shocked. I showed her God's perspective of us humans as stated in Genesis 1. Which book are you reading? Matthew? No, this is Genesis. Page 1 of the whole book. We're equal. God says it right here. This was new information for her.
- "I'm still unsure whether I should keep walking in the ways of [a particular buddhist leader], or if I should dedicate my life to walking in the ways of This Book." This comment was made by a man who's been stopping by the office for years. After all this time, he is still unsure where his final loyalty should lie.
- "Jesus is significant, because He gave His life for people, just like Marx and Lenin...did." Sweet, huh? And absolutely horrifying to westerners. Compare Jesus with Marx? But for the man who said this, it was absolutely the best analogy he could make. He was paying Jesus his highest complement. Very cool.
- "Jesus is significant because He died to take away my sins." A mostly illiterate, former maker of idols grabbed my heart with this statement. Here's this guy who can barely read, and yet, in the midst of others at the meeting who were verbally spar-

ring about philosophy and caste and systemic sins, this guy just quietly spoke about Jesus.

We're excited! And filled with questions. The Lord will lead. Of this we are certain.

Love to you both,
Robin, for us all

The above email makes me laugh. And cry. Steve and I had spent *much time and energy avoiding discipleship?* What were we thinking? To make disciples IS the Great Commission (Mt 28:18-20). We were actively trying to avoid it? How tragic. Thankfully, I also wrote, *We can't stop thinking about it.* What a relief! The Holy Spirit was working in our hearts. We just didn't know it. The Heavenly Gardner was cutting off every branch of ours that wasn't producing fruit and pruning the branches that were bearing fruit so they would produce even more (Jn 15:2).

10 March 2010
Dear Mom and Dad,

Last October, I told you about the school that our friend started for nomads Muslims on the outskirts of Delhi. We have since found out why they live at that location. Years ago, they found an empty lot, stretched some tarp over pieces of bamboo for tents, and have lived there ever since. There is no running water, no electricity. There are no bathrooms. There is no grass. There are no trees. This week, daytime temperatures will reach 100F, and summer has only begun. Today, I visited the community with our friend. He asked me to try to convince the parents that sending their children to his school is important. They claim to value education, but when it comes down to it, attendance has been irregular for most of the children.

Education is important, right? You'd think that speaking about education would be easy for this teacher whose mother and grandmother were both teachers, yet there I was, unsure of what to say. *Learning to read is important.* Really? How? It's easy to say that in achievement based societies that revel in the pull-yourself-up-by-your-own-bootstrap stories, but what about ascribed status societies that don't allow for that? Here, if a person is born a street sweeper, he dies a street sweeper, and his kids will, too, even if they can read. The only hope is a good death which frees Hindus to their next reincarnation, or takes Muslims to Paradise.

I started with a question - Why was education important to them? One lady stated the obvious, "If you go to school, you can learn to read." I asked, "What's so good about that? Why is reading good?" The question stopped her. She didn't know what to say.

We met with the parents in an cement building near the tent community. All the parents sat on the floor, except for the three male community leaders who sat on plastic chairs. I stood in the corner, yelling over the fan that someone had turned on by splicing ancient wires together. After my question, our friend asked a question of his own. Who in the room could read? One man raised his hand. He'd dropped out of school after fifth grade, but he could read. No one else raised a hand, not even the community leaders. This 20-something young man with his 5th grade education is one of the most educated people in a community of 150 families!

I looked at the old man sitting in the plastic chair to my right. Long white beard. Muslim prayer cap on his head. I asked how many children he had. Nine. Did any of them go to school? No. Did he know how to read? No. Another man was the father of six. Some of his kids attend school, but he himself can't read. Another lady has four children, but none attend school. She is also illiterate. What was I supposed to say to these illegal people who are just thankful for daily wages? They are so locked in an oppressive system that there is no hope for improvement. What could I say?

I told them about King Solomon, the wisest king who ever lived. I didn't know if they'd ever heard of him, so I started with his father, David, how he'd been a really good king, and that also Solomon wanted to rule well, but was afraid he wouldn't. So, one day he burnt 1000 sacrifices on an altar. That night, he had a dream. Muslims know about sacrifices. The folks in this community kill a goat every year on Eid. When they heard that Solomon made 1000 sacrifices in one day, they were impressed. He must have really wanted God's help! Muslims also believe in the power of dreams, so it didn't surprise them that God spoke to Solomon that way, but they were amazed by God's offer. Solomon could really ask God for anything he wanted? I asked the parents what they would have asked for. Most said that they'd ask for peace, but when they heard that Solomon asked for wisdom, they all nodded their heads. That was an even better request than peace. Everybody knows when a king has wisdom, the kingdom will be fine.

I ended by quoting one of Solomon's proverbs: *A wise man is mightier than a strong man, and a man of knowledge is more powerful than a strong man* (Proverbs 24:5). Here, from the wisest king who ever lived, is the answer to the question. We send our kids to school so they can learn to become wise.

The parents clapped when I finished the story. They loved it! Heads nodded. They agreed! Yes, our children need wisdom. We must encourage them to go to school! It wasn't until later that I found out that these people had indeed heard of Solomon. They didn't know the details, but they knew he'd been a great king. Leave it to God. He promised to make Solomon's kingdom a great one, and kept His promise to such an extent that even today, thousands of years after Solomon died, people who live thousands of miles from Jerusalem, aren't Jewish, and can't even read, know his name.

God kept another promise today, too. Years ago, Jesus told His followers that He would always be with them wherever they went. I felt that today. I had absolutely no idea what I was going to say to these dear people, but God knew what they needed to hear, and it wasn't some suburban American perspective on improving one's life through good education and hard work. What they needed to hear was the real story of a real man who asked something from the Real God and got it.

How I love you (and am grateful for my education!),
Robin, for us all

21 June 2010
Dear Mom and Dad,

Delhi feels very far away. I am sitting on the sofa in Steve's brother's living room here in the northeast corner of Texas. There is wall-to-wall carpeting on the floor. The shades are drawn to keep out the summer sun. The AC is running. It's cool enough inside that I am wearing jeans, and all of us slept under thick comforters last night.

In less than two weeks, we'll be returning to our India. Are we glad to go? Are we glad we came? As you know, returning to America two summers in a row was not our plan. It is not easy to visit this place. Life in America is (physically) easy compared to India. Friendships here are rich and deep. Seeing you guys and Steve's family is unspeakably precious. When we leave, our heartstrings will tear again, and then we will need to readjust to life in Delhi again. The next few weeks will not be easy ones, yet we know we have to go. No, we want to go. We miss seeing people's faces light up when they hear that there is a good God who made them, loves them, and knows them by name. It is a Message we've heard so often in the west that we take it for granted. In the east, it's a radical concept.

The other night, Steve summarized our life well. He said, "Some people think we work in India because there's so very much work to do, and so few people doing it, as if it's the great need which drives us. It's not! It's not the need. If it were, it wouldn't sustain us very long. We do what we do because God deserves to be known for Who He is. He is good. He is lovely and loving. He is kind. He desires good lives for people. He wants people to walk in freedom, not fear. He is good enough that He deserves for people to know the truth about Him, rather than lies. This is what sustains us - God is worth it."

Love you both,
Robin, with Steve, Eirene, Isabel and Aaron

11 July 2010
Dear Mom and Dad,

Honestly, I can't imagine working with this ministry for very much longer. Even thinking about doing this for one more year is draining. On the other hand, it could be that I'm just exhausted and find it too easy to blame the ministry for my fatigue.

Here's what I'm embarrassed to admit aloud - so many foreigners have left India during the last 12 months that I have begun to think, *OK, God, when will it be my turn to also finally be released from this place?* Isn't that awful? How could I think such a thing?

Now that I've finally admitted it, I know leaving India is not the answer. What I need is Jesus' touch.

Please pray that I get a touch from God. I need to carve out time in my day to sit and hear from Him. I don't do that well. I'm distracted by the stress of the ministry, but also the vegetable seller, fruit seller and the trash guys forever knocking on the door, the maid needing direction, homeschooling Aaron, helping the girls with their homework, the power going out and the heat sucking the life out of me, having no water in the house.

I need to take time to sit and listen.

His touch. That's what I need.

Love,
Robin

28 August 2010

Dear Mom and Dad,

I read earlier this month that this is the wettest monsoon in Delhi in 15 years. Temps have been below 100F since July. We've never experienced such a cool August.

It seemed incredible that, despite all the rain, I hadn't suffered a single mosquito bite for days. Then, it came. Pain. Horrible pain. Started in my back, crept up to my head, then swept down to my feet. Then came the fever. Dengue Fever, to be exact. I have never before felt pain like that. I couldn't open my eyes. Couldn't eat. My platelet count dropped. About Day 7, my hands and feet swelled up like balloons. It was hard to touch anyone or anything. They burned! I couldn't sleep. Out of sheer desperation, I finally paced the house while clapping and rubbing my hands - anything to keep my mind off the burning.

When the pain was at its worst, I made those phone calls. In spite of the miles, in spite of my age and the fact that I am a mother myself, I needed to call you. "Talk to me," I pleaded. You did. You chatted about anything that came to your mind. It was exactly what I needed. You reminded me that God was with me. He knew how I felt. There was purpose even in this.

Finally, the pain began to abate. I could think again. Then came the day I got out of bed and took my first steps down the hall to join the family in the living room. As I did, I looked around and realized that the kids were OK. My family was fine. Kids were doing their homework. There was food on the table. All was at peace.

Thank you so much for your prayers. I can't say that they made the pain go away, lightened the symptoms or shortened the duration of things. Some might ask, "Why even bother?"

The whole time I was sick, our house helper was home suffering her own bout of dengue. Poor Steve did it all. In this land where everything is done by hand, from cooking to washing dishes to hanging up laundry, Steve did it. He also took care of me, remembered all my meds, made lunches for school, drove the girls to school, took Aaron to dance class, oversaw homework, and tucked them all into bed at night, all while assuring them that Mom was going to get better. It may sound trite, but God's grace covered us. Through the fog of my pain, when I couldn't see around me to even care what was going on, God was here. His grace sustained us. His grace was perfect in our weakness, whether it was the weakness of little kids who didn't like seeing their mother in pain, or the weakness of an almost-39-year-old woman who never even felt the mosquito bite.

We felt His mercy and grace through your prayers. Thank you.
All my love,
Robin and all

As I stated in the email dated 11 July 2010, things were stressful in the ministry. On 1 February 2011, we received the following email from a dear friend and prayer partner:

> ...I feel like this month is going to have a 'lighthouse' moment where you [will feel] led to go in one direction, but the moment will reveal to you that you might hit 'land' or something unpleasant. Look out for that moment and take heed, my precious Friends. Wisdom and trust will carry you all through...

Steve responded for us both:

> Your word is significant. Robin and I are thinking and praying about many things these days. Another word to us recently was *patience*. Waiting is hard, yet God is not in a hurry. That is, not until He says "March!" in which case it is time to immediately obey, right?
>
> Thank you for the word and your prayers.

26 March 2011
Dear Mom and Dad,

We moved to Delhi four years ago with no fixed amount of time in our minds about how long we'd stay. We still don't know how long we're supposed to live here. We have no plans to leave, but there are changes coming. Good ones.

Last month, Steve and I spent a lot of time praying and thinking about our roles at the ministry. We also met with leaders in our mission agency who listened well and gave good advice.

Including our time in the mountains, we have lived in India for almost seven years, but neither of us has reached the level of Hindi fluency we desire. We can engage in everyday conversations, and can read and write in Hindi, but we cannot teach in Hindi about social or spiritual truths. We want to. We want to be able to enter low-caste communities without a translator and interact on deep levels with local leaders about spiritual and social matters. Therefore, after much prayer and thought, we now believe that it is time for Steve to hand over his office duties to the Indian staff. For the remainder of this year, Steve and I will focus only on language study.

A good friend recently told us that in his twelve years in India, he's never met anyone who took time off to go deeper with language after living in country as long as we have. Once again, Steve and I just have to do things differently!

We don't plan on fully leaving the local ministry. We're just hoping for a change in roles. We want to begin focusing on what excites us most: making disciples in OBC communities. To do that well, we need more Hindi. We want to encourage and help low-caste people live lives of dignity. We look forward to doing this in Hindi, in about a year.

We are excited about the changes, and thankful that God is directing so clearly. Your prayers have been such a huge help. Thank you. Please continue praying, especially that the staff and we will have God's grace and wisdom to transition well.

Your studious daughter,
Robin and all

29 April 2011

Dear Mom and Dad,

Over the years, we've studied our way through Ephesians, James and Genesis during Friday Bible study at the office. Recently, we started studying Habbakuk. Once we got past the giggles about the strange name, the group was hooked by his story. His country was flooded with corruption. The poor were oppressed. Things were so bad he finally cried out, *How long, Lord, must I call for help, and You will not listen?* The group loved that. It's a prayer many of them echo daily.

The low caste peoples of India understand oppression. Even those who occasionally rise through the ranks are not spared. For instance, last month, the Inspector General of Registration for the state of Kerala, a man of Dalit background, retired. The very next day, government officers entered his former office, and "cleansed" it by spraying holy water on the threshold, and then on the furniture. Later, they went outside and did the same to the government-issued car he'd been driving. What made the water holy? It was mixed with cow dung. Cow dung infested water was cleaner than the man.

Leading Friday Bible study is always a humbling affair for Steve and me. Yes, we're still leading it, even during this season of focused language study. We try to give as little direction as possible, though. When needed, we might provide some background about a passage, but after that, we try to not lead but only ask questions. What does the passage mean to them? What do they think it's saying? We wait to hear their thoughts. They usually surprise and humble us with their insight.

Consider Habakkuk's prayer mentioned above. I think I can relate. I've had days, even seasons, when I felt like God couldn't hear me, or simply wasn't listening, but I have never cried to Him from the depths of despair because "holy" men (the Hindu priesthood) believed that water laced with cow dung was cleaner than my presence.

There is a group of ladies who attend every week. They all live in the same, very poor neighborhood. They were all married to men they didn't choose. The lucky ones finished 10th grade, but some of the women cannot read at all. None of their husbands have consistent employment. Two weeks ago, one of the ladies broke down in tears. Said that she knew how Habakkuk felt, then asked if any of us knew why God was angry with her. She figured that God must be angry about something because, though she's been a disciple of Jesus for three years, she's still hungry. All she has in her kitchen is some white rice.

Another of the ladies wasn't feeling well, so she didn't speak until the very end when she admitted that she wasn't exactly ill. She was trying to recover from the beating her husband had given her the night before. There had been no explanation. No warning. Just beating around her head and shoulders. This lady has followed Jesus for years. Why is He not listening? Why does her husband still beat her?

According to a 2009 UN report, 2 out of 3 Indian wives experience domestic violence. Calling the police doesn't help. More often than not, they don't want to get involved, but if they do come, they usually do nothing more than ask the wife what she did to make her husband so angry. After they leave, the extended family beat the wife again for shaming them in front of the neighbors.

Racism. Hunger. Pain. Injustice. *How long, O Lord, must I call for help? But you do not listen! 'Violence is everywhere!' I cry, but you do not come to save* (1:1).

We had no answers for our sisters, but we tried to honor their pain with silence as they wept. Then, we returned to Habakkuk. We saw that he determined to watch and wait for God's answer, to hold on: *I will climb up to my watchtower and stand at my guard post. There I will wait to see what the Lord says and how he will answer my complaint* (2:1).

Is God as good as we hope He is? Will He answer, if we wait for Him? Is He even able to answer? Can He speak? Is He a figment of our imagination? If I wait for Him, will I be disappointed? These are the questions our Indian friends ask. We wait with them.

Thank you for standing on the watchtower with us for India's low caste peoples, waiting to see how He will answer their cry.

All my love,
Robin, for us all

6 May 2011

Dear Mom and Dad,

Do you remember my 8th grade math teacher? He spent more time explaining why Americans would never fully embrace the metric system than preparing us for algebra. He asked us, how could people who wear *ten gallon hats*, encourage others to *walk a mile in someone else's shoes*, and complain about having a *ton of work* ever accept the metric system? He wasn't a very good math teacher, but his points about the link between language and culture fascinated me. Want to know about a people? Learn their language.

Yesterday, Steve and I made a list of different Hindi words for *god*. We quickly thought of eight. These weren't different titles or synonyms with slight differences. Just god. There are probably more. Next, we wrote all the words for worship. We remembered seven. Again, not different types of worship. Just worship. Gives us an idea of what most Indians consider important, doesn't it?

What about Americans? What do we consider important? There's one word we avoid - toilet. Have you ever counted the many euphemisms we employ for that word? We ask for the restroom, the men's room, the ladies' room, the little girls' room (or the little boys' room). We might say we need to powder our nose or freshen up. We even look for "the john." Poor John. What did he ever do? And what does it say about us that we go to such great lengths to mask the obvious? Here in India, people simply ask, "Where is the toilet?"

Sometimes the opposite is true - instead of many words for something, there is no word. This can be just as insightful. Consider the word *righteous*. The Hebrew word for *righteousness* means integrity, straightness. For the Hebrews, righteous people pleased God with their lives. Noah and Abraham were described as righteous. How did they do it? How did they please God with their lives? Habakkuk makes it clear - *the righteous one shall live by faith*. Noah and Abraham were considered righteous because they believed, they lived by faith. Today, we who follow Christ believe the same. God judges us as righteous, not because of anything we do, but because of what (in Whom) we believe.

The Hindi word for righteous is *dharmee*. It's from the word dharma, which is a person's caste duty. How does a person become dharmee? By doing one's duty. There is no other way. Dharmee is not a way of faith or belief, but duty and requirement. For instance, a Brahmin must put caste duty (dharma) above all else. He must never break caste by doing work of another caste. He must never clean up after himself, sweep the floor, carry out the garbage, or touch a dead body. If he sticks to his own dharma, he is considered dharmee. Likewise, a low caste person must observe the duty of the low caste. If a lowly sweeper aspires to anything higher or better, he is denying his dharma and can never be dharmee.

Dharmee is the accepted word for righteous in the Hindi Bible. Noah is dharmee, so is Abraham. But, they weren't dharmee. They were righteous. They were not bound by obligation and subjugation. They were men of faith.

After this season of learning, we look forward to engaging India's low caste communities in discussions about dharmee and how God has established a different plan for giving righteousness to His children. Pray for us!

All my love,
Robin, for us all

29 June 2011
Dear Mom and Dad,

This month, for the first time in three years, we took a holiday to our old stomping grounds in the mountains. What a treat to see old friends, stay once more in "our" house, enjoy the cool air, and walk familiar mountain trails! We laughed much, enjoyed the quiet, marveled at the fierce rain storms, and avoided the giant spiders. We also reflected on how far we've come. In September, it will be ten years since we first moved to India. A whole decade. Our kids are bigger now (and we have three). We have gray hair.

Ten years ago, we didn't know dal from rice. The giant city of Delhi scared us, we craved juicy hamburgers, and longed to sing familiar, English worship songs on Sundays. These days, we like living in Delhi despite the heat. Our favourite food is Indian. Has 10:00 am chai replaced the blood in our veins? We enjoy singing worship songs in Hindi, and I can't remember when I started utilising British English spellings.

We also know "less" now than we did ten years ago. When we arrived, we we so sure about things. We were here for Steve to use his engineering skills to serve the institutional church. We were going to stay for two years, and we most certainly did not like the plains. Life was hot and crowded down there. Why would anyone live there?

Today, we have no set number of years in our job description. Most of the Indians we know have no connection to the institutional church. Ten years ago, we were too busy doing engineering to focus exclusively on Hindi. Now, it's all we do.

What about next year? We want to take part in reaching India's unreached lower caste communities. They number about 800 million. We have no idea where to even start. Isaiah said it well: *No one has heard, no ear has perceived, no eye has seen any God besides You, Who acts on behalf of those who wait for Him* (Isaiah 64:4).

It's been ten years! What will the next ten bring? God knows. His knowledge is our surety. I pray it will be yours, as well.

All my love,
Robin, for us all

22 August 2011
Dear Mom and Dad,

Thought you'd appreciate a quote from one of your favourites - Henri Nouwen:

When we take a critical look at ourselves, we...recognize that competition, not compassion, is our main motivation in life. Our sense of self is dependent upon the way we compare ourselves with others...we are protective of our "trophies." After all, who am I if I can't proudly point to something that sets me apart from others? This all-pervasive competition stands in the way of our being compassionate. Compassion requires us to let go of differences...to enter into places of pain, to share the brokenness, fear and confusion of our fellow human beings. Yet, we hate pain, suffering and fear, and so we shrink from true compassion. How much easier just to feel general kindness! After all, we can't all be Mother Teresa, now, can we? In the end, we continue with our competitive lives, collecting our trophies, and glorying in our distinctions.*

Steve and I were meditating on these words last week when we got a phone call. A friend wanted to know if Steve would go with him to visit his eunuch friends. Yes, eunuchs. I don't think we've told you about India's eunuchs.

For generations, eunuchs served the Mogul rulers of India. They usually provided protection for the women of the palace, but some served as advisors to kings, and even generals. After the British deposed the last Mogul ruler, the eunuchs had nowhere to go. Palace life was over. No longer valued and trusted, they found themselves thrust into a society which feared them, considered them cursed, and ostracized them. Not much has changed. Today, eunuchs are (at best) ignored, but usually feared. Reviled, even.

Not every person in a eunuch community is an actual eunuch. Some are men who dress and live as women. Others have genital deformities. Children born with such deformities are considered cursed, so they are given to eunuch communities at very early ages to live their whole lives as outcasts.

This was Steve's third visit to the eunuchs. The visits aren't easy for him, but having friendships with outsiders is difficult for the eunuchs, too. They are more accustomed to receiving abuse than kindness, so they don't trust easily. Our friend has spent a lot of time building trust with them. They had called and asked him to come and discuss the Word with them, and pray. Would Steve go, too? Despite his discomfort, how could Steve say no? An invitation from one of the most ostracized communities in all of India is hard to ignore.

After a 90-minute auto rickshaw ride, Steve and our friend were welcomed at the door. Ten "ladies" gathered together in the main room. Our friend prayed, then read from the book of Isaiah about the Messiah. Steve shared the creation story in Hindi. Well, he slogged through it, but they appreciated his attempt. Some of the ladies were sick and wanted prayer. Steve encouraged our friend to not pray for them, but to let them pray for each other. They should not think that there's anything special about us or magical about our prayers. God hears us all. Our friend instructed them to lay hands on those who were sick, and to pray to God and ask for healing. Afterward, they fed Steve and our friend some great food, and then it was done. Steve arrived home even before the kids got back from school.

One day. One city. Two different worlds. Steve spent the morning with human beings who are rejected, hated, feared, and considered cursed. He cannot relate. His family loves him. He's never been the direct recipient of actual hatred. Not even our cat fears Steve! He has absolutely nothing in common with the ladies of that eunuch community. Or, does he? They invited our friend to come because they want the same thing that we all want - to know they're not alone, to know that someone has compassion. They want to feel God's touch. We can all relate to that.

Compassion. We crave it. The angel told Mary that she was to call the Babe, Immanuel, which means *God with us*. Why was that important? The Latin root word for compassion means to suffer with. In order to truly suffer with others, we have to be with others, "walk in their shoes," feel what they feel. Our God crossed the line of distinction between Himself and us. He became Immanuel. He entered into the human places of pain. He suffered with. Thus, He has compassion for us, and He calls us to have the same for others.*

Pray for us, that we'll be people who, like Christ, are willing to cross the line of distinction between ourselves and others, and share in their brokenness so that many more will see that they are not alone, and that God is a God of compassion.

All our love,
Robin, for us all
(* *Compassion: A Reflection on the Christian Life*)

29 September 2011
Dear Mom and Dad,

Another move. Our third move within Delhi in less than five years. Our first two flats were located in a posh neighborhood (as they say here) with a high-end market. Everyone in Delhi knows that market. Living down the street from it made it easy for visitors to find us, but other than that, we weren't especially keen on living there. We'll take thrift stores over brand names any day!

Several months ago, our landlord told us that they wanted to tear down the building and build new. We were out. After viewing many apartments all over town, the Lord in His irony led us to a place literally around the corner from our building. Around the corner, but a different world. It's called M. Village. Yes, village.

When the British ruled India, they constructed a brand new capital called New Delhi. Just adjacent to Old Delhi, they laid out new streets in a grid with designated areas for shopping, government and worship. Nice and organized. Very British. However, when India became independent on August 15, 1947, she split into two parts, India and Pakistan. In the months that followed independence, millions of people were forced to migrate from one country to the other. Muslims were forced off their ancestral homes and to the new Pakistan. Hindus and Sikhs were forced to leave Pakistan and relocate to India. Numbers vary, but the forced migration resulted in 12-14 million refugees. New Delhi received the largest numbers of refugees in both countries. The city doubled from 1 to 2 million in less than a year. Can you imagine one million people being added to Austin in 12 months? Where would they live? What would they do? How would they eat? What if they spoke another language? Suffice it to say, the city's organized planning went out the window.

We still see the effects of the population influx today. Between our new neighbourhood and the center of the city is an invisible line. It's the place where the planning stopped and the quick-build-something-because-the-hordes- have-arrived began. As the city spread over the years, it engulfed entire villages in its wake, like the one where we now live. If you walked down our road, you wouldn't know that you had stepped into a "village," but the locals know. They are quite proud of the fact that their families lived here before Independence.

We like our new neighborhood. No posh market. Our flat is a little less than 1000 sq. feet, and has only two bedrooms. The lanes are often too narrow for cars. There is a mosque a few blocks away that was built in the 1500s, but don't get your hopes up about coming to see it. The neighbourhood garbage dump is right next door, so it's not exactly on anyone's list of Things to See in Delhi.

We've noticed something about our new street. All of our immediate neighbors have the same last name. Our new landlords, the shop owner several blocks down the lane, the school friends across the street, all named Sharma. It is a high caste, Brahmin name. The best we can figure is that this must have been the Brahmin side of the village. Even today, those who live here acknowledge that this is the nicer side of M. Village. The mosque and garbage dump I mentioned are on the opposite side of the neighborhood. Brahmins would have not lived on the same side of the village as the mosque.

As you think of us in our new place, pray that we will live out Jesus' words - *Go and learn what this means: 'I want kindness more than I want animal sacrifices'* (Mt. 9:13). Most religions, including India's brahmanism, believe that outward acts like temple sacrifices and dietary restrictions are more important than kindness. Even we followers of Jesus live that lie. We long for our new neighbors to know that outward acts don't impress God. He wants our hearts.

Love you both,
Robin and all

6 October 2011
Dear Mom and Dad,
    Below is an email I just wrote to an old friend. I thought you might enjoy reading it.

    ....For the most part, only the upper tiers (highest castes) of India's society can afford to leave India. I'd be interested to know the last name of this family you've met. That would tell us where they're from, and probably their caste, too. It is also the highest castes who tend to be vegetarian. They can afford to be picky about what they eat. You are meeting India's wealthiest of the wealthy. That's how they got out.
    About the veg vs. non-veg. thing. It's an issue of definitions. Indians consider eggs to be meat, not dairy. Thus, devout Hindus don't eat eggs, but that doesn't mean they're vegans. They love dairy. Milk is a holy thing. It would bless this family you've met if you took the time to bake something without eggs.
    Also (and I freely admit that I think I know everything), Hindus usually have no problem with Jesus. He was a really good guy. Perhaps He was even a god. Why not? Many gods incarnate. The problem comes with thinking that only Jesus is God. If they say that, they risk offending all the other gods. This fear often disappears when they witness a miracle.
    In our experience, when Jesus heals someone who was sick but didn't improve no matter how often the Hindu family prayed, or when He answers a need that's been worrying them for a long time, then they throw out their idols and give Him their allegiance.
    An Indian friend of ours who was raised a Hindu, but is now a follower of Jesus, hosts prayer meetings in his home. He invites anyone of any faith to attend. When the prayer meeting starts, they ask him who they should pray to. Our friend tells them to pray to whomever they want. He doesn't care. As for him, he's going to pray to Jesus. And then he does. Openly. Loudly. After a while, the others begin to see that his prayers have power and life and get answers, but theirs don't. Soon enough, they start praying to Jesus, too! Our friend doesn't argue with them. He doesn't try to explain that Jesus is more powerful than the

fake gods. He just prays. Remember when the prophet Elijah prayed for God to send fire from heaven? He didn't argue with the prophets of Baal about anything. He didn't need to. They all saw for themselves who was God. Our friend follows that example.

Jesus is not intimidated by people's searches. He is Lord. He can (and does) reveal Himself to those who are truly knocking, even if they're knocking on the wrong door. He can see their hearts.

So, my Friend, keep loving on these folks! Pray that they would have eyes to see and ears to hear. Finally, don't be afraid to be as open with them about your faith as you would with another follower of Jesus. They will not be offended by your honesty. They are not westerners who find these things embarrassing to discuss. Just be you. God will shine through you. He already is.

Blessings,
Robin

November 2011 - June 2016

Fruitfulness!

Those who remain in me, and I in them,
*will produce **much** fruit...*
When you produce much fruit, you are my true disciples.
This brings great glory to my Father.
(John 15)

In 2011, Steve and I attended disciple making trainings sponsored by our mission agency. The trainings changed our lives. For two weeks, we studied only the Word. We didn't read books about missions or study modern patterns in missions. We very simply opened our Bibles and looked for answers to questions such as, Did Jesus have a strategy for reaching lost people? How embarrassing that my first thought after hearing the question was Outreach?!? Did Jesus engage in outreach? I'd always pictured Jesus just kind of going around preaching and healing until He eventually got to the cross. During our trainings, we found treasure hiding in plain sight. For instance, the task of the Great Commission in Mt 28 is not to go teach people about Jesus. *What??!!!*

God used the trainings to shift our paradigms. We used to think that even though the Bible says that God loves the word, He knows most will be lost, so we must be content with only seeing a few saved. We now realized that it was time to stop dismissing 2 Peter 3:9 as hyperbole. God desires that *none should perish*. End of story. Similarly, Jesus' statement about the harvest being plentiful wasn't mere wishful thinking. I was mortified to admit that I had considered many such verses to be exaggeration. After all, we sure hadn't seen much of that plentiful harvest. Maybe Jesus was waxing poetic, or maybe He was out of touch? Poor Jesus. He didn't know any better. But, what if He wasn't delusional? What if He was right about the harvest? If so, then why had we seen such little fruit? Maybe it was time to stop blaming the hard ground for the small harvest and instead evaluate what we were doing - our strategies and our approaches.

Then came the final, ministry-altering question - What if, instead of focusing on what we can do (engineering, teaching, administration, communication), we focus on what needs to be done? In all the years we'd been on the field, Steve and I had concentrated on the skills that we, personally, "brought to the table." What if we'd been missing the point? What if the question had never been about our skills, but rather, What needs to be done in order to save the lost? And yes, the answer to that question would include skills we don't have (befriending strangers, praying with unbelievers, following the instructions given in Luke 10). What a relief to discover in Scripture that our skills (or lack thereof) didn't matter.

Life is not about me and my skills. Obeying Jesus' command in Mt 28 to make disciples doesn't revolve around my methods, personality type or intelligence level. Like with Moses, God is still in the business of using people with speech problems to talk to pharoahs. The pressure is off! Life really isn't about me! Though I had sung the phrase for years, I had lived the opposite by consistently focusing on my skills and abilities.

Peter and Andrew and the rest of Jesus' first disciples were not invited to follow Him because they were the best or the smartest. They weren't born extroverts who just naturally loved people. They were un-educated fishermen, vile tax collectors and oppressed underdogs who obeyed Jesus. Eventually, amazingly(!), they reached the then-known world with the Gospel (Acts 19:10). Could such impact still be possible? Might Steve and I also become more fruitful than we had ever imag-ined?

We now saw that fruitfulness did not depend upon having the most up-to-date programs or money, the quickest wit, best translation abilities or keenest cultural insights. We would become fruitful in one way - by obeying Jesus, simply and literally. In reality, we hadn't even obeyed the most basic of commands! In Mt 28, Jesus commanded His disciples to go and make disciples, teaching them to obey all His com-mands, baptizing them in His Name. Sure, we'd obeyed the command to go, but how many disciples had we made? How many people had we personally baptized? Had we taught people to obey Jesus, or had we only taught them *about* Him?

The training excited and renewed us. For the first time in our lives on the Field, we were focused on God's desire for none to perish rather than our skills and personality traits. We were not designing buildings, serving in administrative roles or teaching. We wanted to do nothing less than make disciples. To that end, we were trying "new" things:

1. Prayer - We began praying like never before. Prayer was no longer just a personal, "devotional time" activity, but part of our job description.
2. Discipling - We no longer separated evangelism from dis-cipleship, but focused on discipling people from the very beginning.
3. Luke 10 - We began to literally apply Jesus' strategies for reaching the unreached.

One day toward the end of December, Steve was walking down our street. As he rounded the corner, he almost (literally) ran into an acquaintance named Sanjay. We had met him at a foot-washing event a few years before, but not seen him since. What follows is Sanjay's de-scription of what happened after *bumping into* Steve that day. I have tried to keep the translation as close to the original Hindi as possible.

I was born into a Christian family. We were a family who followed the Christian traditions. When I was old enough, my father sent me to receive Bible training. I received four years of training, and then was given the job of being a Bible teacher. Over time, I was able to start 17 different churches in rural areas. The churches covered a large geographical area.

Then, in December 2011, I met Brother Steve on the road in Delhi. He asked if I would like to come to his house for training in church planting.

At that point in my life, I was a very proud man. I had a large ministry. I had started a school and a Bible training center. I had done many things, so I was proud. In my heart, I thought, *What can this guy teach me?* I thought I had everything I needed. I knew the Bible. I wondered what would we talk about? What would we do? In my mind, I decided that I would not go to Steve's house for any Bible training.

However, I talked to Steve again in January 2012. I was again in Delhi, this time riding in an auto rickshaw with a friend. I asked him to give me Brother Steve's phone number. I wanted to call Brother Steve and wish him a Happy New Year. When I called him, Brother Steve asked me, "Sanjay, I spoke with before you about a church planting training. Why don't you come?"

I said OK. I would come and I would bring some friends with me.

When we went to Brother Steve's house, I wondered what in the world would we do? But, it was the most amazing thing. He gave us water to drink when we arrived, then he thanked us for coming. Then he gave me a piece of paper and a pen and said, "Today, we are going to study Scripture. I'm going to go make chai for everyone. While I do that, please, all of you, copy Mt. 28:16-20 from your Bibles onto your pieces of paper. Next to the passage, write how you are going to apply it to your life."

What kind of training was this? All he did was give me a piece of paper and a pen!

At that point, I had completed 12 years of ministry. I had Bible college training. I had created this giant ministry/started all these works. But, Brother Steve didn't say anything to me. All he did was go make chai. Even so, in 10 minutes time, I was a completely changed man.

I read in Mt. 28 that Jesus said we're to go and make disciples.

This is what I wrote down on my paper. Later [after sharing with him what was on my paper], Brother Steve asked me, "Sanjay, you have such a large ministry, but do you have any disciples?"

I thought to myself, *I don't have a single one. In 10 years, I have done nothing for Jesus. He said we are to make disciples. Til this day, I have done nothing.*

I remember that the next month, on February 8, I came back to Delhi with a friend to visit with Steve and Robin in their house once more. On that day, we four sat together and studied God's Word. I decided that from then on, I would leave behind all the other things I had started, this big "ministry" that I had created. I returned to my home after meeting with Steve and Robin with one desire - to do nothing less, nothing else, than disciple making. I resigned from the school I had started. I also resigned my position from the international ministry that paid a good salary. I resigned my job as president of the Bible training centre. I left everything. I prayed, "Lord, Your Word says, *Go and make disciples.*" Since that time, I've been focused on obeying this command and nothing else.

I am so happy. Since then, I have come to believe that if all of God's children would only obey His word, they would know joy and God's Kingdom would come to earth.

My younger brother was watching me as I resigned from all the various ministries I had started. He also worked for the same international ministry where I had worked. My father, too, watched me resign from all my jobs. He thought I had gone crazy. He asked, "Where will your money come from now?" Since I had left everything, I no longer had a sure salary. But, even though he (and my whole family, really) thought I was crazy, they also saw how happy I was.

And God provided. I had started a church in my hometown, but it had never been very fruitful. I had poured much effort and energy into this church, had focused on it, yet there were only seven members. Once I began to focus on nothing but the making of disciples, how quickly the church grew! They began to bring tithes and offerings to the worship services. The offerings paid my rent. We had money for food. It was a huge change.

Steve and I had no way of knowing it then, but *fruitfulness* had begun.

31 January 2012

Dear Mom and Dad,

I haven't told you much about our new house helper. She is Hindu, but is very open to spiritual conversations. In fact, Steve and I just got back from her home. This was our second visit to her house to discuss Bible stories. She makes the best chai, a perfect blend of tea, milk, sugar and ginger. Of course, there must always be food with chai, so the table was laden with homemade snacks. We are stuffed!

It's always been hard for us to accept invitations from the poor. They have so little! What right do we have to be a burden by coming to their house? They buy soda for our children that they can't afford, and offer rich foods that are beyond their budget. It makes so much more sense for them to come to our house. We can afford to host them. Also (honestly), visits can be uncomfortable. Culture and language differences make interactions awkward. Our kids chafe at the unwanted attention. We don't want to drink water or eat something that might make us ill. We want to avoid arguments about faith. Why go?

The training that Steve and I attended last year has caused us to rethink pretty much all of our notions about life and ministry, including this one. In Matthew 10 (and also Luke 9 & 10), Jesus commanded His disciples to go out, and to take nothing with them, not even an extra shirt or extra money. They were simply to go. Along the way, when they were invited to stay in someone's home, they were commanded to accept the invitation, to eat what they were served, and to tell the host family about His Kingdom. Never once in those passages did Jesus say to worry about being a burden.

So, we're going to her house these days. You know what? She doesn't see us as a burden. She is honoured by our visits. We have been wrong about many things.

During our visit today, we asked, "Is there anything in your life that you're grateful for today?" It was a tough question. Cultivating gratitude is not a typical concept for most Hindus. Life just is what it is. Next, we asked about troubles. Was there anything going on that was causing them or someone they know to be stressed or troubled? That had an immediate answer. A relative who lives nearby has suffered pain for years. She's a widow. No money. She definitely has troubles.

We asked, "Is there anything that you as a group can do for her? Is there any way you can help her?"

Silence. We could see them digesting the question. Finally, someone said, "We could pray for her." How insightful! There is little concept of interceding for others in the Hindu context.

I asked, "Would you like to do that right now?"

"Could we? How would we do that? What would we say?"

"Anything you want to say," Steve and I said, but they wanted to hear how we would pray for this woman. We kept insisting that they could pray any way they wanted. There is no right way. Finally, I said, "When I pray, I just tell the Father what's going on and what I want Him to do about it." Then, we sat and waited.

There was no way Steve or I was going to lead out in prayer. This family does not need us setting some kind of standard for prayer. After several seconds, the husband started speaking to God out loud, eyes wide open, as if he were talking to any of us in the room. When he began to ask God to make things right for this lady, his sons echoed his words. The wife, our house helper, echoed his words. Steve and I echoed his words. He kept going. A sentence or two later, we all echoed his words again. Then, it was done. It was beautiful.

We are grateful for the five years we served in the ministry here in Delhi. We learned so much! Now, we feel that the time is right for us to step into ministry for ourselves. During all our years here, we have always served under someone. Please pray for us as we step out of the shadows.

The task is huge. Millions of people have never heard the name of Jesus. Not once. Thankfully, the Father is drawing people to Himself. Please pray that God will lead us to more households like our house helper's. Pray that those households will become churches, and that quickly those churches would make other churches.

Love you much,
Robin, for us all

26 March 2012
Dear Mom and Dad,

I'm thinking about our house helper tonight. Did I ever tell you that when we returned to her house for the second Bible study, we heard that their relative had been completely healed of all sickness and pain? Isn't that amazing? God is awesome. She's on my mind tonight because the days of fasting that Hindu women must perform this month is taking its toll on her. Hindu men don't ever seem to fast. It's always the ladies. Wives fast for their husbands. Mothers fast for their sons. It's never the other way around. Such a misogynist system.

During one of her fasting days last week, she asked me for a cup of chai. Talk about unusual! She must have been really tired to ask for such a thing. I had forgotten she was fasting, though, so was almost offended by her request, but then decided that taking offense would be dumb. Why make that choice? The kids and I had made a (really good!) chocolate cake the day before. Maybe she'd like that? Why not choose to bless?

Yes, I am self-centred enough that I need to perform these mental gymnastic in order to serve tea to my house helper. How sad is that?

Finally, I poured chai into a cup, put a slice of cake on a plate, and told her the snack was ready. She took the tea, then reminded me she was fasting.

"Oh, yes, of course. I'm sorry. I forgot, I said. You'll eat at sundown, though, right?" She nodded.

"Great! Then I'll just put the cake in this plastic bag for you, and you can eat it later." She seemed pleased.

As I was putting the cake in the bag, I was trying to think of how I could turn this conversation toward the Lord and freedom from religious rules. Finally, I said, "You know that God looks on our hearts not our stomachs, right?"

She smiled. It was a confused smile, though. It was one of those you're-not-from-here-so-I'm-not-sure-I-heard-you-correctly-just-now-when-you-were-speaking-your-accented-Hindi smiles. Then she said, "Doesn't look at our stomachs? What?"

I tried again. "Well, God looks at our hearts, right? He cares about what's in there. He doesn't really care about what's in our stomachs. Right? I mean, why would He look there? What's in there will just eventually just go 'out'. Right?"

This time she smiled a real smile. Then she asked, "Do you ever fast?"

I explained that there are times I do fast. If there is something I need to pray deeply about, then I'll forgo food, but I do not fast according to a rule or regulation. She understood, and nodded her head. The conversation was over.

We humans want God to care about what's in our stomachs. Religions abound. Each group claims to know what will please God and what won't. Cover your head. Don't cover your head. Grow a beard. Don't grow a beard. Eat certain foods. Don't eat certain foods. Celebrate this holiday. Don't celebrate that one. When will it end? Jesus addressed this issue of legalism. The religious leaders confronted Him one day because His disciples didn't fast or pray the way they thought His disciples should. When they asked Jesus about it, He responded by quoting the prophet Isaiah: *These people show honor to* [God] *with words, but their hearts are far from* [God]. *Their worship of* [God] *is worthless. The things they teach are nothing but human rules* (Is 29:13).

We long to see the oppressed peoples of the subcontinent freed from their burdens of tradition and human rules. Please pray that we will never promote mere religion or human rules.

Loving and missing you,
Robin for us all

8 July 2012
Dear Mom and Dad,

Greetings from the Delhi! It was so nice to see you this summer, but it feels good to sleep in our own beds again and see the friends who mean so much to us. It's still crowded here. Still dirty. It's so hot that the start of school was delayed by one week. Specifically, it was 110F in the shade every day this week, complete with high humidity. At one point, Steve and I had to attend a meeting in a room with no AC. The ceiling fans whirled until the power went out, then we just sat in our plastic chairs, sweat pouring off our faces and down our backs. After an hour, I looked down and saw that my feet looked like fat sausages. Toes were all pudgy and swollen. We decided it was time to go. The Indians didn't leave. They stayed for three more hours. We are American wimps.

Do you mind pretending with me for a moment? Let's say you're the head of a non-profit that serves children with disabilities in a country where that's unique. Finances are tight. You haven't paid your staff for three months. You owe rent. Your landlord wants his property back. Along comes a rich politician who says, "I'd like to help you out. I know a way to keep your organization financed for a lifetime. I will give you $18 million. Cash the check, then secretly give 40% of it back to me in cash. You'll get your desperately needed funds. I'll get a large tax write-off plus untraceable cash 'under the table.' No one will be the wiser, and the children will be helped." Would you be tempted?

Our friend Gia lived this scenario last week. She was so tempted to say yes. No one would ever know. This type of thing happens daily in India. All government officials get kick-backs. She could do such good work with the money. If she doesn't take it, the official will find another non-profit who will. We were so proud of her for saying no. God will provide for her somehow. He will bless her for choosing integrity over money.

So, we're home. We miss you already, but oh, home is good.
Love,
Robin and all

By August 2012, we were working more and more with Sanjay. We weren't using the term *partner* yet, but we were beginning to feel like teammates, and glad for it. God had another member for our team, though. An unexpected gift from China was headed our way.

Phoebe was a single lady serving with our agency in China, and one of the only foreigners in her city. She spent her days managing a coffee shop, and was so deeply embedded in her community that she went days without speaking English. We met during the disciple making training in 2011, and "hit it off" almost immediately, as if we'd been friends for years. We sat together during the sessions and discussed the content each evening. We prayed for each other. We ate every meal together, explored the city, and drank more and various types of milk tea than we knew existed. Along the way, we realized that we in India and she in China had spent a lot of years doing a lot of things, but hadn't made disciples.

After the training, the emails started flowing. God was speaking to her about her life and ministry. Had we ever considered having a teammate? Would we be willing to consider her joining us in India?

Phoebe visited in the summer of 2012. She met Sanjay, his top level leaders, and his congregation. She got some sense of what life in Delhi would look like. We talked and prayed, and decided to be a team. Phoebe had details to finalize, but finally arrived in Delhi in the spring of 2013, and has been our teammate ever since. Actually, more than teammate, Phoebe is friend and confidant, prayer partner, and "aunt" to our kids. A true co-laborer in life and ministry. We are grateful God saw fit to bring us together, and I am humbled by His generous goodness. You see, back in 2011 when I attended those trainings, internally I was "kicking and screaming" about being separated from my children for two whole weeks. Meanwhile, God had this gift to give us, to our whole family and the work. How gracious of God to ignore my complaints and protests so that we could meet Phoebe. What we all would have missed if the Lord had listened to me!

12 August 2012

Dear Mom and Dad,

Many traditional Christian ministries in India - hospitals and orphanages, for example - have a building for worship somewhere on the property. The ministries hope that the local townspeople will be so touched by the love and care found at the mission, that they will, one day, join the congregation. It's a bit like that old movie *Field of Dreams* with the *if we build it, they will come* idea.

For the last year, Steve and I have been comparing that approach with Scripture. Did Jesus ever tell anyone to build anything? We don't see it. When He did send His disciples out, He instructed them that if they met someone who was willing to host them, they were to go into that home, pray for the sick and preach the Kingdom.

Two weeks ago, I visited with Sanjay and 14 disciple makers to discuss this idea of reaching out to others. At one point, I asked, "Why do you think Jesus told His disciples to go into people's homes? Why would He say to do that?"

They thought for a while. Finally, one man said, "I guess so they could get to know people. You don't really know people until you see them interacting with their families in their homes. It's hard to hide your true self at home."

I agreed. That was a good point. Were there any other ideas? They thought for a while, but no one had anything else to say. They all agreed that they liked that answer. What else could it be? I then asked, "OK, tell me this. If a muslim came to your town and built a really pretty, really nice mosque, would you enter it?"

They looked offended and a little befuddled. "No," they said, "that wouldn't be right."

"Would you feel comfortable in that mosque?"

"No, certainly not," they said.

"Yet, we go to villages and build church buildings, and expect the villagers to be so happy to come to our building. Why would they come? They feel as uncomfortable in our buildings as we feel in theirs."

I continued, "We like our buildings. We feel comfortable in them. We sit in our favourite corner every Sunday. We know all the songs. We know all the people. We know what to do when the collection bag is passed. Our neighbours don't know what to do. They don't know the songs. They don't know where to sit. Why do we make them feel uncomfortable? We should own the discomfort. We should go to them, to their houses where they have their own favourite corners and where they know everybody. After all, when you think about it, isn't that what Jesus did? He owned the discomfort by coming to earth where we are. He didn't expect us to go to Him."

Silence. Shock. Smiles to mask confusion.

I pushed further by apologizing. I said, "The model for ministry you follow, you learned from us. We westerners brought the if we build it they will come model when we came to your shores with all our money, and built our big hospitals and church buildings. That wasn't Jesus' model. He never built a building or invited anyone to a synagogue. He went to people's homes. It's easy. It's cheap. More importantly, it puts the listeners at ease because they are, literally, in their home turf. Please forgive us for giving you a poor model for ministry. Please stop copying us. Please follow Jesus' model."

At the end, I gave the leaders two weeks to go out and try putting Jesus' model into practice. Steve will travel out there this week to hear how it went. I'm looking forward to having some interesting stories to share with you!

How we love you both,
Robin, for us all

23 August 2012
Dear Mom and Dad,

Steve and I were feeling lost this morning, not sure what to focus on today. We finally decided to study some of Jesus' parables with this question in mind: What Kingdom principle concerning reaching the lost does this parable teach? I thought you'd enjoy hearing about what we learned.

We read the parable of the mustard seed becoming a tree, and also the one about yeast leavening a batch of flour. After a long time of prayer, an obvious truth hit us- the sower knew he was planting a mustard seed. He knew what would happen. He fully expected that the small seed would one day become the largest thing in the field. Likewise, the housewife knew what she was doing when she put yeast into the flour. She fully expected the yeast to do its work, to leaven the whole batch. Both of these people believed in and expected big outcomes. If the yeast hadn't done its work on all the flour, the housewife would have been disappointed. She would have hated the waste of time and effort. She would have resented having to go out and buy new yeast, or whatever it was that women did back then to get yeast. Meanwhile, if the mustard seed hadn't grown into the largest thing in the field, the farmer would have felt cheated. These people were expecting big things.

A small seed becomes a huge tree. A small amount of yeast affects the whole batch. God's Kingdom grows in the same way. If we don't see it happening, then it's right for us to evaluate what we're doing. Perhaps our methods are wrong. Perhaps it's time to shake the dust off our feet and move to a field that's ready for harvest. We can and should ask God about it, listen for the answer, and then change as necessary.

We feel watered by this Word. Just wanted to share it with you.

Thanks for listening,
Robin

29 October 2012

Dear Mom and Dad,

Meeting with our house helper and her family has been inconsistent lately due to scheduling conflicts. A few days ago, it finally occurred to us that, though we can't get to her house, she comes to our house everyday. We could teach her a Bible story here, and then she can go home and share it with her family. They could discuss it, and then she can tell us how it went. We asked her about the plan. She said, "I'd love to do that!"

Today we met for the first time. Steve made chai for the three of us. As soon as we sat down, the doorbell rang. It was our friend and translator. He visits often, so our house helper knows him. He was an unexpected gift to the discussion.

First, I told the Bible story:

One day, Jesus told a story to some who had great confidence in their own righteousness and scorned everyone else: "Two men went to the Temple to pray. One was a Pharisee, and the other was a despised tax collector. The Pharisee stood by himself and prayed this prayer: 'I thank you, God, that I am not a sinner like everyone else. For I don't cheat, I don't sin, and I don't commit adultery. I'm certainly not like that tax collector! I fast twice a week, and I give you a tenth of my income.'"

"But the tax collector stood at a distance and dared not even lift his eyes to heaven as he prayed. Instead, he beat his chest in sorrow, saying, 'O God, be merciful to me, for I am a sinner.' I tell you, this sinner, not the Pharisee, returned home justified before God. Those who exalt themselves will be humbled, and those who humble themselves will be exalted."

Our house helper asked about the tax collector. What exactly did he do? Our friend explained how he was like officials here - corrupt, taking bribes, living richly off the poor. Our house helper was confused. "He did bad things, yet he was the one who was forgiven?"

I asked her if she remembered how the religious leader prayed. "Oh, yes, full of himself," she said. When she realized that it wasn't what the men did, but the attitude of their hearts that made them forgiven and right with God, she became very quiet.

Next, we acted out the story. Steve and our friend played the parts. I narrated. After that, we took turns re-telling the story, from memory, together. After the fourth time through the story, the implications hit her. She said, "If everyone lived this way (believing that those who humble themselves will be exalted and those who exalt themselves will be humbled), there would be no problems in the world." Then, overwhelmed by the beauty of Jesus' perspective, our house helper wept.

She told us that religious leaders say that God doesn't care for her or her family because they are of low caste. She also faces this prejudice daily from her employers, our landlords. She's cleaned their floors for years, but she's still not allowed to touch the furniture. She pollutes what she touches. The grandmother watches over her as she cleans to make sure she doesn't touch anything important. When she needs a rest, she must sit in the stairwell, never inside their apartment. Yet, here we were, sitting on our furniture, drinking chai that Steve (the husband-and-head-of-home) made, hearing that in Jesus' Kingdom those with humble hearts are elevated.

Valuing humility? Our house helper had never heard of that before. A verse in Proverbs says that a soft answer turns away wrath. Not here. In India, a soft answer is considered permission for the wrathful one to keep going, even stronger. Our helper knows this. She said, "But, those hard-hearted people (our landlord) will never believe anything like this."

Our answer was that next week, she will hear a story about a changed heart - Zacchaeus, the tax collector. She left smiling. She's going home to tell the story to her family, and discus it with them. We can't wait to hear about their discussion.

Love,
Robin and all

28 February 2013

Dear Mom and Dad,

January was a blur. On the third, we began the search for a new flat. Again. One month later, we unpacked the last box in our new place. Our new home is within walking distance of the kids' school.

The day after we moved in, we hosted our first guest: Sanjay! We were overjoyed to hear some of the testimonies. Families are being changed.

Recently, I was online searching for statistics about India. Here's an interesting one: The National Family Health Survey found that 51% of Indian men and 54% of Indian women found it justifiable for a man to beat his wife.* Over 1 billion people live in India. That's a lot of people who think it's OK for a man to beat his wife, and is the context for the following true story.

One of the lay leaders was literally obeying Jesus' strategy as found in Luke 10. He and a partner visited a village where they had never been before. They met a family who were interested in hearing a story about the God who made the world. The two men stayed in their home for the afternoon. The men didn't preach, but simply shared a Bible Story, then asked questions about it, including the most important one, *If this Story were true, how would you apply it to your life?*

The family enjoyed the discussion. They asked the men to return again, which they did. The meetings became regular. The neighbours began to notice. They began hanging out near the door and windows. They liked hearing the Stories, too. One such neighbour, a lady, entered the house. She sat and listened to the Story. She liked the discussion. She liked the prayer. She began attending regularly. The problem was, her husband didn't like her going to these meetings. He beat her after each one. He had no job. He was drunk all the time. She kept attending the meetings in spite of the beatings. Finally, one day, she looked at her husband and said, "Fine. You don't want me to go to these meetings? I won't go. But first, you have to attend a meeting with me, just one time. If you don't like it, when it's done you can beat me again. But, at least go one time."

He got drunk first, but he went. He fidgeted. He glared at the leaders. He left in a huff. But, when it was all over, he didn't beat his wife. The next week, he attended the meeting again. This time, he wasn't drunk. When the meeting was done, he told the leaders that he wanted to follow the God of those Stories. He was tired of drinking all the time. He wanted a new life. This family is now changed. The husband no longer beats his wife. He stopped drinking. They are learning the Stories. Their lives are new.

A true story of a changed life. A woman had the courage to tell her husband, "You want to beat me? Go ahead, but at least come to the meeting!" It's even more amazing when you consider what the *Upanishads* (Hindu holy texts) say about women:

> If she does not give in [to any man's sexual advances], let him, as he likes, bribe her (with presents)...if she... does not give in, let him...beat her with a stick or with his hand, and overcome her, saying: 'With manly strength and glory I take away thy glory' (Brihadaranyaka-Upanishad 6:4:6-7).

This story is not unique. We have a notebook full of similar testimonies. Whole families are being changed as they hear the True Stories about God, and then apply the Stories to their lives.

So, go ahead. Google the statistics. It's not pretty. But, God is here. He is changing families. He will change India, one family at a time.

Your hopeful daughter,
Robin, for us all
(*http://www.bbc.co.uk/news/world-asia-india-17398004)

In 2013, the final member joined our Team - Sanjay's brother, John. Below is Sanjay's description of how his brother came to join us in the work. I have tried to remain as close to the original Hindi as possible.

During the first year that I worked with Steve and Robin, my younger brother watched. Though he was receiving a good salary from an international ministry, he wasn't happy. He was stressed all the time. After that year, I asked him, "Brother, would you like to join me in the work?"

He said, "You seem so happy."

I urged him, "Come work with me!" I described what God was doing. He said yes, and then resigned from the international ministry (and assured salary).

During all the years before working with Steve and Robin, back when I had been so busy with all my big ministry endeavors, my family hadn't really been with me. We had not been in unity. Now, though, my brother and I were working together to make disciples.

I was glad to work with my brother. I knew I needed partners.

It wasn't good to be making disciples alone. I remembered the story of when Jesus called Andrew to be His disciple. Andrew immediately went and got his brother, Simon (Peter) to come and meet Jesus, too. The Lord is using both of us together in the same way He used Peter and Andrew.

4 April 2013
Dear Mom and Dad,

The other day, I was thinking about that story in John 4 when Jesus met with the Samaritan woman. Talk about a woman with problems! She had married and divorced 5 times, and was now living with a man who wasn't her husband. That's a lot of marriages, but since we know that women in first century Palestine didn't have the right to leave their husbands, we know that this woman wasn't just divorced. She was rejected. Five times over. The current man hadn't even bothered to go through with a ceremony. What pain she must have harbored in her heart!

Jesus meets her. He has a need (thirst), and He allows her to meet that need by giving Him a drink. They have a conversation. At the end of their discussion, she runs back into her village (where everyone knew her history), and she says to them, "Come, see a man who told me everything I ever did. Could this be the Messiah?"

What I love about this story is how little the Samaritan woman actually understood about Jesus. After their conversation, she had one testimony - "Come, see a man who told me everything I ever did." She didn't say, Come, see the Man who claims to be God, or even, Come, see the Man who is the best teacher I've ever heard. Perhaps she didn't even know that Jesus could do miracles. What she did know was this - Jesus knew her, inside and out. That's what she proclaimed to anyone who would listen.

I have witnessed a similar testimony. This morning, I met with our former landlord's wife. Each Monday, I meet with her to discuss a Truth Story. Today was the first time that one of her neighbours joined us. As soon as the she sat down, I got a nervous. Would the neighbour understand my accented Hindi? Did she even want to be there, or was she joining to be polite? Would she argue, or would she discuss (there is a difference!)?

The former landlady and I have established a routine. We start with chai and chit-chat. Then, I pass her the story to read. I could read the story. In fact, I love to read Hindi aloud, but the landlady likes to read even more than I do, and since her accent is better (smile), I don't argue. Today was no exception, but as soon as my former landlady finished reading, the neighbour began talking. It was as if she had no desire to discuss the story at all. She just wanted to talk about how hard her life is.

I didn't know what to do. Should I stop her? We weren't there to hear her whine. How was I supposed to steer the conversation back to the creation account?

All of a sudden, the landlady began to speak. She is no scholar. To date, she has heard a total of three Bible stories. Yet, there she was, sharing with the neighbour about all she has learned from applying those three stories to her life. She talked about the peace she feels in her heart, now that she, like Mary, Martha's sister, is choosing to sit at God's feet each day and be with Him.

There is so much my former landlady doesn't know. What she doesn't know didn't matter. Like the Samaritan woman, she simply shared what she knew - You've got to believe me, even spending two minutes at God's feet has changed me.

And I? I sat and watched, listened and prayed. It was beautiful and inspiring. And humbling. The neighbour said that she wants to return again next week so she can feel the peace she felt today during our time together.

Love you both,
Robin and all

1 August 2013
Dear Mom and Dad,

I've been thinking lately about the first time I studied Proverbs 25:21-22: *If your enemy is hungry, give him bread to eat; and if he is thirsty, give him water to drink; for in doing so, you will heap coals of fire upon his head, and the Lord will reward you.*

I had been having trouble with a friend. I can no longer remember any of the actual circumstances of the situation, but I remember how excited I was when I read this passage. Here was the answer! I knew that as a follower of Jesus, I couldn't actively seek revenge on my friend. This verse seemed to offer something better than revenge - shame. The way I read it, if I did good to those who didn't deserve it (my enemies), then God would somehow use my act of goodwill to shame them. How cool of God to provide a loophole, a way to get back at others without actually breaking the "take no revenge" command!

Over the years, I began to understand that my 7th grade interpretation didn't harmonize with what I saw in Jesus. I couldn't think of a single time when He performed a good deed in order to shame anybody. After reading in John's gospel that Jesus didn't come to condemn (shame) anyone, but to save everyone (Jn 3:17), I was more confused than ever. What does it mean to heap coals on someone's head, if not for shame?

Throughout the nine years we've lived in India, we have witnessed the ramifications of the teachings of karma. The essence is that you get what you earn. Period. Karma dictates all and cannot be changed. If I only get what I deserve, then there is no room for, no need for, compassion. I must have done something bad to earn the bad thing that has happened to me. End of story. The poor must have done something bad in a former life to be struck with poverty now. A person who suffers an accident must have somehow earned the accident. The sick are sick because they earned the illness. Karma even dictates blessing. If I'm sitting at the top of the system, then good for me. I must have done right things in a former life to earn this good place, otherwise I wouldn't be here. I am entitled to my nice house, my AC, the service of others, the best schools for my children.

Here's my confession - being kind to people who feel entitled to it is not easy. Time and again, we are tempted to be kind in order to shame. Here's a typical "Robin" thought - *My neighbours are never going to sweep our shared stairwell, so I will, and they'll see me sweeping, and feel so ashamed for not contributing that they'll change. After all, God promises that my good deeds will be like coals of fire on their heads! I hope they feel really bad!!!*

Consider this footnote from the Amplified Bible:

This [proverb] is not to be understood as a revengeful act intended to embarrass its victim, but just the opposite. The picture is that of the high priest who, on the Day of Atonement, would take his censor and fill it with coals of fire from the altar. Then, he'd put incense on the coals to create a sweet-smelling fragrance. The smoke of the incense would then be acceptable to God for atonement (Lev 16:12).

Oh. Of course! Of course this is what God would want from my good deeds. My doing good to even my (supposed) enemies is not to bring shame upon their heads. I am to do good to those who don't deserve it in order to be an agent of redemption.

Pray for me as I learn to walk in Jesus' steps. After all, *The Lord is good to everyone. He showers compassion on all his creation* (Ps 145:9).

Still learning,
Robin and all

31 August 2013
Dear Mom and Dad,

We met with Sanjay yesterday. He told us about a woman named Sunita. I'd like to share her story with you. Like many (most?) women in India, she was married young to a man her parents chose for her. The good news is that he has a job. The bad news is that whatever money he makes goes straight to alcohol.

A few months ago, Sunita was crying during the Sunday worship service. Sanjay asked what was the matter? Through her tears, Sunita admitted she was tired of being beaten by her alcoholic husband. She also said that since all the money goes to alcohol, she and the children are hungry. There's no money for food. The church gathered around and prayed for her, and then Sanjay asked if there was any way she could make some money. What about setting up a roadside food stall? Sunita admitted that, yes, she was good at making momos (the Tibetan version of Chinese dumplings), but she couldn't afford to buy a steamer.

With joy, Sanjay told us yesterday how the church pooled their money to buy Sunita a momo steamer. Sanjay's church is poor. The small building where they meet for worship has only half a roof. Most of the members live in one-room homes. In fact, many of the women live in the same circumstances as Sunita. Yet, they gladly pooled their money until they had the necessary Rs1500 ($23.00) for her to buy a steamer.

Today, Sunita's husband still drinks. However, Sunita has set up a momo stall outside the door to her one-room home. She makes between Rs400-600 ($6.00-9.00) each day. Also, out of sheer gratitude, she is paying tithe off her earnings back into the fellowship of people who helped her when she so desperately needed it.

I share a lot of bad news about India. Unfortunately, there's a lot of bad news to share. The value of the rupee is falling. Foreign companies are fleeing India's suffocating bureaucracy. Violent crimes against women are rampant. Someone even started a non profit agency to help living people prove they are alive. It seems there is a problem with relatives reporting family members as dead in order to steal their property.*

It's easy to forget that God is here. He is working. He doesn't shake His head, throw up His hands and wonder what to do. Rather, *the Lord looked and was displeased to find there was no justice. He was amazed to see that no one intervened to help the oppressed. So he himself stepped in to save them with his strong arm* (Is 59:15-17).

God is still in the business of stepping in and saving. Please join us in praying for the Sunitas of India. As they are liberated, whole communities will be liberated, and then the nation!

All my love,
Robin, for us all
(*http://www.bbc.co.uk/news/world-asia-india-22685924)

21 October 2013

Dear Mom and Dad,

The following is an entry Steve wrote for a friend's blog:

My family and I have lived in India for over nine years. Our children feel more comfortable here than America. Even my wife, Robin, realized just a short while ago that, due to all the moves she and her family made when she was growing up, she will soon be able to say that she's lived in Delhi longer than anywhere else in her life. Some think we must really like it here to have lived here for so long. We never quite know how to respond to such comments. Do we smile and nod in agreement or be honest and admit how hard it can be? The food is fantastic, of course, and my wife loves the clothes, but India is crowded and hot. The air smells of sewage. There is trash everywhere. The government is a caricature of democracy. Here are two quick, sad statistics:

(1) According to the UN High Commissioner for Human Rights, India has the highest number of street children in the world. No one knows exact numbers. Conservative estimates suggest about 18 million children in India's major cities of Mumbai, Delhi and Kolkata.*
(2) The level of child malnutrition in India is higher than some countries in sub-Saharan Africa. According to experts, 25% of the world's children are underweight. In India, the number is 43%*.
(*http://robertlindsay.wordpress.com/2011/07/22/india-hell-on-earth/)

Do we like it here? There are days when we feel overwhelmed by the darkness, the injustice and oppression, the hopelessness. We only have to open the newspaper to find honour killings, dowry deaths, wealthy politicians who oppress others for the sake of their own pockets, Christian churches who plan large events to celebrate their own anniversaries but don't give to the poor down the street. Meanwhile, here we are, reading the paper in our 1200 sq ft flat that overlooks two parks. Where is the justice? There is none.

Sometimes, Robin and I feel like we're drowning in this ocean of sadness. After all, we're talking about a lot of people. Millions and millions of people. A billion, even.

It's easy to contemplate the road of disbelief. The "well, maybe there isn't a God after all" argument can be pretty compelling in the face of injustice. Maybe atheists are correct? But, if there is no God, if this life of faith is just a myth, then there is absolutely no possibility of redemption for any of it, and that's the bleakest road of all. Then all truly is hopeless. Nothing will ever make sense. No wrongs will ever be righted. And so, we come back, like Peter, and say, *"Where else am I going to go, Jesus? You have the words of life."*

What we have discovered is that every time we come back, He lets us find Him. Or, He finds us. However that works. Personal testimonies are often the antidote. When we catch a glimpse of God working, intimately, in the life of a fellow human being, then we remember that anonymous generalities make God seem absent. Looking at a collective, as in *all* the poor or *all* the oppressed, God seems lost. But, when we hear individual stories of how God is encountering people on personal levels, our faith is renewed. He is alive! He does exist! He is working, intimately, in the affairs of men, women and children all over this planet. We're so grateful we get to live here, with our front row seats. We know so many individual stories. He is good. He does see. He does rescue. Even us. He rescues even us.

Peter wrote, *we were not making up clever stories when we told you about the powerful coming of our Lord Jesus Christ. We saw His...splendour ....with our own eyes* (2 Pet 1:16). There is something about being an eyewitness to His glory. India is a dark place. Who likes darkness? But, that's not the end of the story! We have seen people healed physically. We've seen the demonized freed. Just last week, we saw over 84 brand new disciples baptized! Many of the new disciples were whole households who decided, together, to become followers of Jesus. God is alive, and He is awesome.

Grateful for your love which has helped sustain us in the darkness, Robin, for us all

5 November 2013

Dear Mom and Dad,

Yesterday we celebrated another Diwali, though it wasn't quite the same as celebrating last year with you. None of us will ever forget the fireworks shooting off every roof and balcony without regard to trees, electrical wires, parked cars, or people, including your grandson who almost got his hair burned off his head. This year, we decided to get out of Delhi, so we Smiths-and-Phoebe drove the three hour trip to Sanjay's hometown for a working holiday. Nothing unusual in that. We conduct trainings all the time, right? Except that this was the Very First Time we've ever met with both first and second generation lay leaders! Disciples have made disciples. They are bearing fruit! Each of the original group of disciples whom we trained back in 2012 now has more than one disciple. Some have several.

On the final day of our trip, we visited Sanjay's family home out in the village. Sanjay's brother, John, and his family live there with the parents and their youngest sister. Water buffalo are tied right outside the door. The "modern" cookstove (a 2-burner camping cookstove) was out of gas, so they cooked lunch the village way - up on the roof, over a fire made with cow patties. Best chicken curry we ever had. The kids sucked sugar right out of the cane. The rice was harvested from their fields. We listened to our kids speak Hindi with the family. Best Diwali ever.

We miss you guys. We also, absolutely, love what we do.

Love from afar,
Robin for us all

20 December 2013

Dear Mom and Dad,

Over the last 18 months, Steve, Phoebe, Sanjay, John & I have facilitated 34 trainings for pastors and lay leaders in seven cities across North India. The training sessions are simple. We ask, "Did Jesus have a strategy for reaching those who were far from Him?" We compare Scripture with typical practices and strategies employed today. We evaluate to determine whether our approaches are Biblical commands or mere Christian tradition. We've been privileged to see hearts adjust, hopes expand, and expectations for fruitfulness increase as people realize how simple and fulfilling it is to apply Jesus' strategies to daily life.

Since July 2012, more than 200 new churches have started in places where previously there were none. Many have already planted other churches, some even three generations of churches! Over 400 new followers of Jesus have been baptized. Thank you for your love and faithful prayers.

Thanking God for all He is doing,
Robin and all

3 February 2014

Dear Mom and Dad,

The last time we talked on the phone, I tried to explain about the disciple making trainings that we lead. They tend to be one or two-day events to which we invite followers of Jesus to study Scripture with very specific questions in mind. We ask questions such as:

- Did Jesus give us, His disciples, strategies for reaching the Lost?
- Did Jesus establish patterns for ministry that we can follow?

We apply the answers that emerge from Scripture to our lives and ministries.

Finally, if one picture is worth one thousand words, then perhaps the following pictures will explain better than any report I could write.

No chalkboard. No white board. No Smart Board. No laptops. What they do have matters most: attentive hearts and a willingness to apply.

We provide Bibles and writing supplies for those who can read. White paper taped to the wall makes a simple "blackboard." We purposefully keep things simple so that the process is easy to replicate.

No kids' program. No toys. No playground. No snacks. It's January, but no central heat. No iPod for entertainment.

Worship time! Percussion is the only instrument. Singing is loud and heartfelt, and usually off-key to our western ears.

For this particular training, the roof was the kitchen and dining room. They cooked all the food on a 2-burner stove connected to a tank of gas. The chapatti dough is in the foreground.

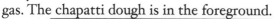

Food is served! In January, the roof is the warmest place in the building. No tables. No silverware. Pieces of the chapatti serve as "spoons."

These cow patties were drying over in a corner of the roof, kept on hand just in case the gas ran out.

The wonderful truth we're learning is that what we have (or don't have) doesn't matter. The most important thing is that we take Jesus at His

Word and apply it. One man from this group planted 22 churches last year! What God needs is our willingness.

May we all become less so He can become more,
Robin, for us all

3 March 2014
Dear Mom and Dad,

What joy is in my heart! I can't wait to share a recent story with you. First, do you remember what Peter said about Jesus in Acts 2:33? *Now He is exalted to the place of highest honor in heaven, at God's right hand. And the Father, as He had promised, gave Him the Holy Spirit to pour out upon us, just as you see and hear today.*

Just as Peter said all those centuries ago, Jesus is still pouring out His Spirit upon His children. The following is a true story.

In January of this year, Raj Haroon, one of Sanjay's main leaders, was visiting a house church in a nearby village. As he walked through the village on his way to the home, six young, strong men grabbed hold of him, beat him, then dragged him to a nearby house and locked him inside. Somehow, Raj Haroon was able to escape and return home. For three weeks, he did not return to that village. He was afraid. He never wanted to visit there again.

As Raj Haroon was praying during that third week of self-imposed exile, he heard the Lord say, "Go back."

He recoiled, "No, Lord!"

The Lord said, "It is time."

Raj Haroon obeyed. As he walked tentatively through the streets, he kept his eyes peeled for the young men. Would they find him again? Finally, he entered the home of the local church. Safe at last! The worship service had already begun. He walked to the side of the room opposite the door, and sat down. Imagine his terror when, a few minutes later, he looked up to see all six young men standing at the door. They looked right at Raj Haroon. They began walking toward him. There was no escape. Fear gripped him until, one-by-one, those young men got down on their knees before Raj Haroon and begged his forgiveness. During his three week absence, they had all become disciples of Jesus!

After the service, Raj Haroon spent time with the young men. None of them were from that village. Within weeks, they all returned to their homes and started churches in their own households. Raj Haroon told Sanjay, "My enemies have become my friends. They are helping me with the work. God has completely changed them. The ones who beat me now see me as their leader. Amazing work! In this way, God is helping us, and I give him all praise. Amen!"

Isn't that beautiful? Please join us in praying for more of God's *amazing work*.

Your joyful daughter,
Robin, for us all

11 April 2014
Dear Mom and Dad,

I've got another story for you today that I know you're going to love. One of the lay leaders is a young man named Satish. He's planted churches in several villages, including one in which a retired army colonel and his family live. The colonel's son is about the same age as Satish, but because of the colonel's connections, the family is one of the wealthiest in the village. The son had time on his hands. He spent his days lifting weights, bulking up. He loved being fit, as they say here. Even so, he became ill. They tried everything: doctors, medicine, prayer to idols, sacrifices and offerings, pilgrimages to holy sites. Nothing helped.

Time passed. One day, the young man told his mother that a person of faith (Satish) was routinely coming to their village, meeting with others in a local home for worship.

"You should go see him," his mother said. "Maybe he will pray for you."

The young man obeyed his mother's suggestion. He attended the worship service. Satish prayed for him in Jesus' Name and he was healed! Soon afterward, the mother also became a disciple of the God who healed her son. She informed her husband, the colonel, of her decision. He flew into a rage. Grabbed his rifle, aimed it at her, and pulled the trigger. He didn't just threaten her. He actually pulled the trigger. He missed. The bullet flew right past her head. So, he improvised. He flipped the rifle around, took hold of the barrel, and swinging it like a club, beat his wife without mercy. He broke one of her legs and severely injured the other.

During the long period of her recovery, this woman performed her daily chores by pulling herself along by her hands. Her broken leg was in a full cast, from toes to thigh. Her other leg couldn't support any weight. Even so, she never stopped talking to her husband about Jesus. He hated it. She kept at it. Finally, she declared, "Kill me if you want, but I know Jesus is truth." After one year, the colonel finally believed. He, too, became a disciple of Jesus.

Today, that woman and her husband have turned their home into a building of worship. Each Sunday, 90 people gather in their home to worship Jesus. She also works with Satish. To date, she has planted seven other house churches.

As families are changed, villages change. And then the nation! May it be, Lord!

Love from afar,
Robin and all

29 May 2014
Dear Mom and Dad,
We were hoping that the process of renewing our visas this year would be easy. Some years it is. Not this year.

(Immigration officer to Steve) "If you are a volunteer with a non-profit, why doesn't your visa say Volunteer on it?"

(Steve) "I don't know. I told the Consulate that I am a volunteer. That's the visa they gave me."

Steve's answer didn't satisfy the man. Not surprising. The immigration office doesn't seem to actually communicate with Indian Consulates overseas. How could we know why they gave us the visa they did? He's the officer. Why doesn't he know? He asked other questions, scribbled on his paper, mumbled unhappily, then told Steve to come back in two weeks. There was to be an inquiry.

It took nearly three weeks to complete the inquiry, at which point they declared, "This will be difficult for you. You have been in India too long."

What? We had to face the prospect that our time in India could be coming to an end. Of course, Steve and I know there will eventually come the day when we leave. May we become un-needed as soon as possible! Leaving now felt too soon to me. I was as stressed as I have ever been. We love our work. The kids are doing great. They love their lives here, their friends. We begged God to let us stay longer.

Two days ago, we returned to the immigration office for a follow-up interview. We were anticipating more difficulties, but all of a sudden we realized the paperwork was moving forward. Five hours later, we left with our new visas. Praise God!!

I don't know why God allowed the process to take so long this year. Here's an interesting development, though - the same day we received our visas, Mr. Modi was sworn in as India's new prime minister. He is the head of the BJP, India's openly Hindu political party. The BJP is one arm of a radical Hindu movement seeking to establish *Hindutva* (Hindu ideals) as the supreme rule of thought/practice/law in the subcontinent. I'm not making this up. You can read about Hindutva on Wikipedia. Pretty crazy stuff.

The BJP is not the only organization to ascribe to Hindutva. On the front page of Sunday's paper, there was a quote from the leader of a sister organization. About Modi's rule, he said he's expecting to see *...a Ram Temple... built soon under the Modi-led regime...[and] Legal prohibition of...religious conversions is a necessity to ensure peace and well-being of the society.*

God allowed us to get our new visas on the very day Modi was sworn in. If their agenda is to build a temple to Ram and make conversions illegal, then we'll pray for God's Temple to continue to grow, and for many more to be born again into the Kingdom of God in the year to come.

It's also been good to have this very clear reminder that we don't just live here. We are on mission. May we always live with the exit strategy in mind.

We love you, Mom and Dad.
Robin, for us all

6 June 2014

Dear Mom and Dad,

I thought you'd enjoy reading this excerpt from the official newsletter our mission agency sent last month.

"Be Quiet, Pastor!"

With surprise and joy, Pastor Sanjay heard these words from a woman in his church in India. Over the last two years, Pastor Sanjay has witnessed over 1000 baptisms and the birth of over 200 churches. The numbers astound us (and him!). Our team in India who trained Pastor Sanjay declared, "We can truly say that all we have done is follow Jesus' ministry strategies and obeyed His commands instead of following traditional methods and strategies for ministry."

In most traditional Christian worship services in India, women do not speak. They hold their children and keep them quiet. They sit separately from the men. They faithfully keep their heads covered in the presence of God and the male leaders. [However, since the team trained Pastor Sanjay and others to obey Jesus' command to make disciples, which includes women], things have changed. Women now read Scripture during worship services. They are learning how to make disciples. They are encouraged to share stories about Jesus with their neighbours and to pray for others. They are even starting churches on their own! An 18-year-old, unmarried woman has started two different house churches. In this male-dominated society where an unmarried girl has no position or authority in a family, modern ministry methods state that women cannot be effective. Yet, this young woman has started and is leading two groups of disciples. We are seeing Jesus perform great feats as all His disciples-men and women- take His words in Matthew 28:16-20 seriously and obey them.

So, Pastor Sanjay was visiting a group of Jesus' followers. He started to share the story of David and Bathsheba. Before long, one of the women spoke up, "Sit down, Pastor. We know this story, so let us tell it to you." Then, she and the other ladies narrated the entire story. Pastor Sanjay was thrilled. What a change from the norm, where women are (at the very least) sidelined, but very often beaten and oppressed just as they are in most of Indian society. Our team once read an essay written by an Indian pastor explaining the biblical argument for husbands to beat their wives. In contrast, here was Pastor Sanjay hearing women say, "We've got this!" These women are now sharing stories with others. Some have planted churches. Some have even seen multiple generations of churches start. All without Pastor Sanjay's involvement!

Oh, that thousands more women (and men) would say, "Be quiet, Pastor! We've got this!"

We love and miss you,
Robin, for us all

29 June 2014
Dear Mom and Dad,

Steve and I have recently been meditating on a 2000-year-old reality: Jesus only needed three years to fully train His disciples. Three. During that time, He expected the disciples to do things. They didn't just sit in the pew or study. More than once, Jesus sent them out to heal the sick and preach the Kingdom without Him (Luke 10). He commanded them to give hungry 5000+ people something to eat (Mark 6). At the end, He told them it was good He was going away. Without Him there, they'd be able to rely on the Holy Spirit. They would do greater things than He had done.

Last month's visa issues reminded us that we do not know how long we'll be allowed to live here. Are we raising up leaders who will also do more than we have done? Do we agree with Jesus, *It's better for you if I go?* Do we willingly share authority in this work? If we had to leave tomorrow, would the work continue without us?

Like Jesus, Paul also invested in others and then left. He was constantly on the move. At one point, he told Timothy, *What you have heard me teach publicly, you should teach others. Share these teachings with people you can trust. Then they will be able to teach others these same things* (2 Timothy 2). Paul didn't hoard insight, knowledge or strategies, nor did he want Timothy to. He instructed Timothy to willingly share what he'd received. This "pay it forward" idea is a critical element in making disciples.

What about us? For the last two years, we've worked closely with Sanjay. We pray together, study the Word together, and together apply God's truth to our lives and ministries. Since Truth is not to be hoarded, Sanjay shares what he learns with a man named Arvind, who then shares with others, including a disciple named Mani. Mani, in his turn, shares with Prakash. Here's the chain:

Sanjay —> Arvind —> Mani —> Prakash

Many such discipleship chains have begun over the last two years. Disciples are pouring into others, who are then pouring into others, but the relationships are not exclusive. In the chain mentioned above, Sanjay mostly shares with Arvind, but he doesn't consider Prakash unworthy of his time. Meanwhile, Mani isn't intimated if Prakash wants to speak with Arvind or Sanjay. We know this because recently Prakash called Sanjay and asked for his help. Would Sanjay accompany him to a nearby village to help him connect with the people? Sanjay willingly agreed. Upon their arrival, the two were shocked to hear villagers greeting each other with the traditional Christian phrase: *Jay Masih ki* (praise the Messiah), rather than a more typical (Hindu) phrase *Ram Ram*. What was going on?

The villagers told Sanjay and Prakash that a Christian ministry visited their small village about 12 years ago. They assigned a local person to be the pastor, and began paying him a salary. His main job as pastor was to enroll the area's poor children into the ministry's Christian boarding school which was located in another town. The pastor knew nothing about Jesus. No one poured into him. He didn't even own a Bible.

Here in India, many people greet others in the name of the god they worship instead of saying hello. Most Christians follow this cultural practice. Thus, when the new pastor heard the ministry people greet each other with Jay Masih ki, he began to do the same. The villagers quickly learned that if they responded in kind, their children's chances of being accepted into the boarding school improved. Unheard of! A village comprised almost entirely of idol worshipers greeting each other in the name of a Messiah they did not know?

With joy in their hearts, Sanjay and Prakash shared about the Masih with the people. They prayed for many. People were healed. Some were freed of demons. Two entire families decided to follow Jesus and were baptised. Prakash is following up with them. He will share with them the Truth he knows, and expect them to share what they learn with others.

Thank you for pouring into us. We are here because of you. The chain continues.

Humbly,
Robin, for us all

29 July 2014

Dear Mom and Dad,

Money and generosity were the main topics in a recent leaders' training. Most of the leaders are poor. They are usually the receivers of generosity. We studied to find the answer to this question: *Are the poor excluded from Jesus' commands to be generous?* The Lord both challenged and encouraged all of us as we studied His Word for the answer.

Toward the end of the day, people were milling around, chatting in small groups. One of the groups seemed disturbed. I went and asked what was troubling them. They pointed to one member of their small group and said, "Brother Chand's church is already applying the truths we studied today. They are amazingly generous. They have no money, but every week, they bring what they have to the worship service - rice, wheat, or vegetables - and they share the fruit of their labours with each other. In fact, they give so much food each week that Chand is able to make some money to pay for his family's needs by selling the extra at the market."

I said, "That is wonderful! You are taking God at His word and obeying Him! So, why the downcast faces?"

"Chand's wife is five months pregnant, but she is extremely ill. She can hardly get out of bed. Her medicine costs 1500Rs ($25US) per week. Chand told us that he hasn't eaten for the past four days. He's been selling his portion of the family's food at the market, hoping to make enough money to pay for the medicine."

I could not speak. What need. What love! With heavy hearts, we gathered around Chand, prayed for his wife to be healed, and for Father God to meet their every need. We took up a collection to help his family. The group gave enough money to cover four weeks' worth of medicine, a generous offering for these poor laborers, but not enough to cover the remainder of the pregnancy. Chand needed a miracle.

Three weeks later, I learned that soon after we prayed, Chand's wife was completely healed of her illness!

God is awesome!
Robin and all

2 August 2014
Dear Mom and Dad,

Monsoon rain is so refreshing. Most of the year, this city is dirty, polluted, dusty. Monsoon showers are a profound relief. All five of us sigh deeply. We open the windows and balcony doors. We relish the cool breeze and breathe the wet air. My shoulders relax, I sit in the cross breeze and thank God for refreshment.

Keep that picture of refreshment, of cool breezes after weeks of stifling heat, in your minds because it's how we feel about the following story. There's so much bad news in India. It's easy to get discouraged, to think that people's hearts will always be hard, that maybe the darkness is just a bit too dark for God to find anybody. Rejoice with us as you read this month's letter. The darkness is not more powerful than the Light!

Steve and I recently heard about an illiterate, Dalit woman. She is a street sweeper in her village. The government of India employs Dalits to sweep streets all over the country, and that is what they do. Literally. They are outfitted with brooms, and each day they go outside and sweep streets by hand. In March, this woman was sweeping the streets of her village. It was hot. She became thirsty after working for a while, but she was sweeping the street where the high caste people live. No way would they give her something to drink. She put down her broom and walked over to the street where her caste people live. She knocked on a door. A man answered. Sure, he'd give her some water. He invited her inside to wait. She stepped through the door, then noticed a woman sleeping in the main room of the home. This is unusual. Women in India, especially in the villages of India, do all the work in the house. They awake before dawn, and only sleep after the rest of the family is already in bed. Yet, here was a woman sleeping in the middle of the day! She asked the man about it. He said that the woman was his wife. She had been sick for 15 years. He had taken her to many doctors and hospitals, priests and holy places. Nothing had worked. All that money spent. All that time. Here she was, still sick.

The Dalit woman is a follower of Jesus. She had been a Christian for many years, but just recently heard a "new" teaching concerning Matthew 28 and Luke 10. A visiting teacher had shown from the Scriptures that before Jesus left the earth, He commanded His disciples to be, not merely believers, but active disciples. He instructed them to make other disciples, to baptize them, and to teach them to obey Him. The visitor also mentioned Jesus' instructions to go into people's homes, pray for them and talk about Him. The woman listened intently. No one had ever told her that such activities were for her. She'd always been taught that baptizing, praying and going were for important people like her pastor, people with degrees, or at the very least, people who could read. She couldn't even do that.

Now, here she was, in the home of someone with a need. She'd knocked on a random door, looking for water. What if this hadn't been random after all? She asked the man (Jagdish), "May I pray for your wife?"

Jagdish asked, "What does 'pray for her' mean?"

She said, "I'd like to pray to God for your wife."

Jagdish said, "OK."

It sounds too good to be true, right? It gets better. The sick woman got up. She was healed. Illness gone. All better.

Jagdish and his whole family were so grateful that they joined the woman for worship the next Sunday. They declared themselves to be followers of this Jesus, the One who was powerful enough to heal. The visiting teacher was there that week, too. You might have guessed that he is John, Sanjay's brother. After the service, John also prayed for Jagdish and Jagdish's whole family. As of the writing of this email, she is still healthy. The illness is gone.

Jagdish is so happy! He's sharing the news with everyone, including his extended family. His sister lives in a different village with her husband and his family. She didn't believe Jagdish. He insisted it was true. She finally said that she wanted a blessing, too. Would Jagdish bring the woman-who-prayed to her house? He did. The two went and prayed for Jagdish's sister and her family in their village. The sister's husband (Jagdish's brother-in-law) was so touched that he began sharing about these things at the school where he works. Some of his co-workers were so impressed that they asked for prayer, too. The brother-in-law is now connecting the school folks with Jagdish and the woman-who-prayed!

An illiterate woman who sweeps streets for a living decided to take God at His word and pray for someone. She didn't call the pastor. She didn't discount herself because of her inabilities. She prayed. God healed. The family believed. As they shared about the wonderful thing that happened, others were infused with their joy and hope, and now the Good News is spreading to yet more villages.

The darkness is powerless to stop the Light. The darkness can never overcome it!

We wish you could be here to rejoice with us.
Robin, for Steve and the kids

1 September 2014
Dear Mom and Dad,

I've never paid much attention before, but the first disciples did a lot of traveling.

- Peter visited *the Lord's people who lived in Lydda* (Acts 9:32).
- Paul and Barnabas traveled. (*Let us return and visit the brethren in every city in which we proclaimed the word of the Lord, and see how they are,* Acts 15:36).
- Timothy traveled. (*But I hope....to send Timothy to you shortly so that I also maybe encouraged when I learn of your condition,* Phil 2:19).
- Paul told the church in Corinth - *Here for this* third *time I am ready to come to you, and I will not be a burden to you...* (2 Cor 12:14).

We find it hard to believe that God has done so much work in the last two years that we are now *visiting brethren* to see how they are. Two weeks ago, Steve, Sanjay, and John spent three days visiting churches in rural India. They visited seven different villages in two districts (counties). They personally met with 70 of the 90 active disciple makers in those areas. Most lead at least one church, but many are leading two, three or four churches! Two years ago, only a small handful of disciples lived in these districts. Now, there are 90 people actively labouring in the harvest fields, and each one is bearing fruit!

The people are poor. They eat what they are able to eke out of the ground. Most cannot read. However, nearly all of them have experienced miracles of healing and/or deliverance. They go and tell others what Jesus has done for them, and then pray for others in the same manner that they were prayed for.

We're thrilled by all that is happening. We also know that God wants to do more. His heart is so big! He doesn't wish destruction on anyone, but wants to save everyone (2 Pet 3:9). Please keep praying.

Love from your excited daughter,
Robin, for us all

_____

PS - Enjoy the photos....

New Delhi is the second largest city in the entire world. Even so, 70% of India lives in the rural setting. How long would it take to count 70% of a billion? The numbers boggle the mind.

Above - a farmer's wife
Below - a gathering of house church leaders. As is typical in most villages, some of the women completely cover their faces with their saris.

Below - a house church. The floor is made of a mixture of cow dung and mud.

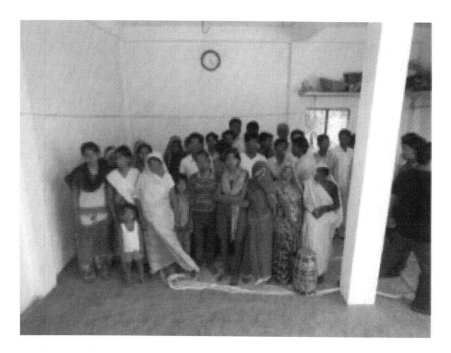

Villages often have electricity for only a few hours each day. Below is a leaders' meeting. They sat on the roof in the cooler air (100F) and read by a gas-light.

Not all of India is rural. Below is a typical day on the Women's Only car on the Delhi metro (subway).

25 September 2014
Dear Mom and Dad,

Steve and I are reading a book these days called *The Insanity of Obedience*. At one point, the author quotes a leader of a house church in China who differentiates between mere church members and true followers of Jesus:

> Of that large number of believers...two-thirds of them are what we would call "members"....[they] attend a house church. Most...have been baptized [and]...contribute financially to the work of a house church. But we do not consider church members to be true followers of Jesus until they have led other people to Christ and...have helped plant more house churches.

This man's perspective caused us to wonder, *Are we mere church members or are we true followers of Jesus?* A friend of Sanjay's named Suresh is a true follower. When we first met him, he had no vision beyond pastoring his small church here in Delhi. However, through studying the Word in our trainings, Suresh has been challenged by the command to make disciples, not just believers. Last week, he told us about a widow named Bija that he'd recently met.

Bija has four children. Widows all over the world carry great burdens. India is no exception. Hinduism decrees that a husband and wife are "one," which isn't as romantic as it sounds. In the Hindu perspective of one, the husband's life literally becomes the wife's life. If she is widowed, her life is considered over, even though she still breathes. Thankfully, widows today are seldom burned on their husband's funeral pyres, but their lives are bleak. They are often kicked out of their in-laws' home. Why feed the widow? Widows can never remarry. They must live chaste, quiet lives of service until they can finally die, and hopefully be reborn something better than a woman.

When Suresh met Bija, she told him about her life: kicked out by the in-laws after her husband died, was trying to provide for her children by selling vegetables on the street. High inflation was keeping sales down. An issue with her thyroid was causing serious health problems which prevented her from working. There was no money to feed her four children, no medicine. She invited Suresh to come into her home. He reported later that when he walked into Bija's home, he felt overwhelmed by depression and hopelessness. They were almost tangible. He began to pray. He made no promises of health or wealth to this widow, but prayed. Bija's children were also there. He read to them from the Bible. They prayed and sang together. He left after an hour, burdened. Had his visit accomplished anything?

A few days later, Bija visited Suresh. With a smile, she reported that she felt better than she had in a long time. She was healthy enough to work again! Furthermore, customers were buying, even though prices were still high! She was like a new woman. Her neighbours noticed. They had been watching her and her children. They knew of her plight. These sudden, drastic changes were so amazing that seven families had begun attending a Discovery Bible study in her home in order to learn more!

Praying that we pursue nothing less than insane obedience,
Robin, for us all

24 November 2014

Dear Mom and Dad,

Last week, Steve, Sanjay and John made another trip to visit the churches. They spent the first night in a local leader's home. The man is one of four brothers. In proper Indian fashion, he and his brothers and their families all live under one roof. Steve called me that night. I asked him about all the background noise. He said, "Robin, I am, literally and completely, surrounded by people." That God sent us two introverts to work in one of the most populated countries on the planet is proof of His sense of humor, as well as His commitment to make us like Jesus, who was, undoubtedly, the perfect balance of introvert and extrovert.

The second day was a repeat of the first, until Mandeep arrived. Mandeep had attended a few trainings back in 2013. Back then, he didn't contribute to discussions, but sat in the back. After a few sessions, he stopped coming. It happens sometimes. Some people are ready to let go of tradition. Others are not.

The surprise that Steve, Sanjay and John felt upon seeing Mandeep after so long was quickly replaced by shock as they listened to his story.

Mandeep had been a pastor of a small congregation for a while by the time he attended his first training. His church consisted of 8 people. He was somehow surviving on Rs1200 per month (about $19.00). At Sanjay's urging, he attended those few trainings. Then, he went home and simply began applying what he'd learned. Today, Mandeep has 60 leaders in a discipleship network! His finances are doing better, too. He now earns Rs3000 per month from the tithes and offerings in the churches. He doesn't keep it for himself, though. Mandeep is generous. He now gives away the same amount he used to earn. Each month, he gives Rs1200 to one of the key disciple makers in his network.

Disciples are making other disciples. In a way, every day is a Thanksgiving Day!

Missing you, especially, this time of year,
Robin, for us all

28 January 2015
Dear Mom and Dad,

Below are the bullet points from the 2014 End of Year Report Steve recently shared with our financial and prayer partners. Rejoice with us!

- December 2012 - 70 churches and Bible studies.
- December 2013 - over 250 churches and Bible study groups had been birthed in several states in North India.
- July 2014 - 850 total churches and Bible study groups. Some of the churches were 4th and 5th generation churches (Sidenote-This deep generational growth means that this work is not dependent upon one person's personality. The Holy Spirit is

growing His Church as followers of Jesus simply obey His commands to go out and make other disciples.).

- January 2015 - Current number of churches and Bible study groups is 1,000.

God truly and sincerely loves the whole world. He doesn't want anyone, *no one*, to perish. We rejoice! We also know it's a drop in the bucket compared to what He still wants to do.

Love,
Robin, for us all

30 January 2015
Dear Mom and Dad,

I'm feeling a bit lost this month. Not sure what to share. I've said it before, the news here isn't good:

According to UNICEF, about 50% of India's population goes to the bathroom in the open.* There are women all over this country who can only "go" during the early morning before dawn or late at night after the sun sets. Can you imagine not being able to go to the bathroom during daylight hours?

Only 1 in 4 Indian homes has a fridge.** Can you imagine not having a refrigerator in your kitchen? It's hotter than 100F for much of the year in this country!

An estimated 400,000 children die in India every year from diarrhea.***

Every day, five people in our city die in road accidents.*^ Everyday. Most are pedestrians and/or motorcycles because there are just too many people walking the streets or weaving through traffic on their bikes.

India is ranked 8th on Forbes list of global multimillionaires, yet the World Bank states the India is home to 1/3 of the world's poorest people.*^^

Sometimes, I wonder what in the world are we doing here? Earlier this month, Steve and I took a day to pray and fast. We needed to be with God. We got quiet. We admitted how we were feeling. We asked Him to give us some direction, to tell us what He would like us to do. That's the precious truth about being a mere servant. The servant doesn't have to worry about all the many things she isn't doing. The servant just has to do the one thing the Master has instructed. We were seeking the light yoke, the easy burden.

At some point that day, we read the parable of the three servants (Mt 25:14-28). Each servant is given some money, and then the master leaves. He's gone for a long time. When he comes back, he checks to see how the servants did. Turns out that while the master was away, the first two servants invested his money. They were good stewards of what they'd received. He tells them both, *You were faithful with little. I will now put you in charge of much*. The last servant didn't do a thing with his money. The master threw him out and gave his small amount to the servant who'd made the most.

It's not a new story, but this time, after reading it, we asked ourselves, "What are our 'bags of gold'? What has God, our Master, entrusted to us?" The answer came: our three main disciples/co-labourers are our bags of gold. Investing in them is how we will be good, faithful servants. We don't need to concern ourselves with things *too great* for us (Ps 131:1). We don't need to be burdened by the bad news. We just need to be faithful with these three. What a relief! What a light burden.

As you pray for us this year, please pray that Sanjay, John, and Suresh will become more fruitful than we ever could. Paul eventually overshadowed Barnabas. It was how it was meant to be. Pray that our relationship with these guys follows the same pattern.

There's still bad news out there. It's a relief to know that carrying it isn't our job.

Love from afar,
Robin and all
(*http://www.bloomberg.com/news/articles/2014-08-03/india-s-toilet-race-failing-as-villages-don-t-use-them)
(**http://www.bloomberg.com/news/articles/2014-08-03/india-s-toilet-race-failing-as-villages-don-t-use-them)
(***http://www.unicef.org/india/children_2357.htm)
(*^http://www.cseindia.org/content/delhi-tops-country-fatal-road-accidents-and-number-pedestrians-and-cyclists-falling-victim-s)
(*^^http://timesofindia.indiatimes.com/india/India-ranked-No-8-on-global-list-of-multimillionaires/articleshow/39708900.cms) (http://www.telegraph.co.uk/news/worldnews/asia/india/10003228/India-has-one-third-of-worlds-poorest-says-World-Bank.html)

1 March 2015
Dear Mom and Dad,

Recently, we received a generous donation from a church in America to buy bicycles for some of the main disciple makers. Having transportation will make it much easier for them to visit with their churches. Below are John's translations of their thank you notes. Enjoy!

My name is Prashant and my father's name is Mr. R. I live in [a fairly backward, rural area of north India]. I am feeling very happy to write this testimony in Christ. I belong with a very poor family. I do not have my own House. I live with my Leader [the man who is discipling me].

Two years ago I knew about Jesus Christ through my leader R.S.. I was born in Hindu family and we were very strong idol worshipers. One day, we all heard the word of God by Brother R.S. and I read the Holy Bible. After that we realized and confessed our all sins which we have done in our previous time. We were very sad with those gods because we were doing idol worship and fasting, but we did not have peace in the life.

After that, I decided that as I was saved by someone, I will also go and I will also try to save someone in Jesus Christ. Last year, I started to share the gospel with different - different people and areas. I am working in three villages which are 7, 9, and 11 kilometers from my house. Some villages has transport facility and some have none. Sometime I was asking bicycle from my neighbors and friends to reach to those places, but now I am very happy and I can go now to more distant villages and now I can use my self more [be more effective] with this help [of the bike]. I did not see you [I have never met you], but I am very thankful for you to provide me new bicycle. I pray to God he use you more for his Work and bless you and your family.

Greetings to you in Jesus' name. My name is Kishore and my father's name is S. We are from [the foothills of the Himalayas].

I was born in very squalid area. By birth, we were idol worshipers, but three years ago we knew about Jesus Christ through a teacher who came to our area. They taught us about real love of Christ. He came this world, He crucified himself for our all sins. We realized Jesus is a very loving Lord, and finally we decided to become His follower. After this we felt very peaceful in our souls and our personal life, and then I decided I will also go to new people for sharing this message with those people which is feeling same pain as I had before.

I was working in many different areas, but I did not have any vehicle and I belong with very poor family. The work of my father is litter's [They sort through trash, gathering paper and plastic recyclables to sell in the market. It is one of the poorest and lowest castes in India].

I was not very strong financially, and it was very difficult to purchase new bicycle for me, but now I am very happy and thankful for you to provide me this wonderful gift and now I can work more with it.

[Note: Kishore is from a very low-caste background. He and his household pray for miracles and share the Message among the unreached. They have planted many churches and started many Bible studies in their area, even though most of them are illiterate. They listen to audio Bibles to grow in their faith.]

Rejoicing!...and missing you,
Robin and all

4 April 2015
Dear Mom and Dad,

Tomorrow is Easter Sunday. Today is the hidden day of Easter weekend. The Gospels don't mention Saturday. Thursday was the Last Supper. On Friday, Jesus was crucified. What was Saturday like? None of the disciples knew that Sunday was coming. When they saw the empty tomb, they were only confused. That it was empty didn't convince them He was alive. No one was looking for Sunday. I wonder, how sad was Saturday?

Steve has a photo of three illiterate, Indian women, all married to poor farmers. Each woman, along with her whole family, has become a follower of Jesus during the last three years. Like many of the disciples in the movement, these ladies know that Truth is not to be hoarded or defended, but shared. Question is, how to do that if they can't read?

We distribute rechargeable speakers with SIM cards in illiterate communities. Each SIM card has recordings of Bible stories on it. Each of the ladies in Steve's photo has a speaker. To share a story, all they have to do is press play. After each story, they ask the same, simple questions each time: What does this story teach about God? What does it teach about people? How can we apply the story to our lives? By following this simple method, these three illiterate, poor women are currently leading 40 house churches! Their obedience puts us learned (over-learned) rich, westerners to shame.

Some question the faith of disciples in house churches such as these. How can their faith be deep? They aren't led by someone trained in a seminary! No daily dose of Oswald Chambers? No .com to google? No 45-minute weekly sermon?

In Acts 2:36-47, we see that healthy churches are generous and meet others' needs. Today, the new churches these women have started are being obedient to the same Spirit. Steve and I recently learned that some of the brand new churches, comprised of very poor people, are generously giving of their own finances to start a literacy project in their community. In a country where most ministries and churches seek outside funding for any and every activity, these poor farmers are using their own funds. The new disciples are quickly learning to be generous and to love their neighbours in very practical ways. It confirms the depth of their faith. God is at work in these days, among these peoples!

What about Hidden Saturday? I'm guessing that the disciples believed what Jesus said, that all was truly finished. He was gone. Dead and buried. Sometimes I feel stuck in "Saturday." Corruption here exists at every level of society. Women of every economic level suffer oppression. Infant mortality rivals subsaharan Africa. Local religions call evil good, and good evil. Then, we meet women like the ones in the photo. We see the same Spirit in them that was in Jesus. Dead Man coming back to life? Illiterate women leading Bible studies? Impossible!

This is God, our God! The God of the impossible. The same yesterday, today and forever. Oh how we love our front-row seats.

Loving you from afar,
Robin and all

16 May 2015
Dear Mom and Dad,

It has been three years since we last came home to America. We're excited and nervous. Four months in the States. We haven't spent that much time in the US since 2006!

Last Tuesday, we took the day off and drove out to visit Sanjay and his extended family in the village. Several of their family members have birthdays in May, so everyone gathered for one giant celebration.

As guests, we Smiths and Phoebe were given the best seats in the house: the bed in the main room. The kitchen was too hot, so the ladies moved the 2-burner camping stove out into the central room of the house where there's a 5x5 foot ventilation hole in the roof, kind of like a permanently opened moon roof on a car. That's also where the water pump is located. Sanjay's dad was modern enough in his thinking years ago to give his family "running water" by putting the pump right in the centre of the house. They placed the stove on the floor. Ladies were hunched over it, stirring pots. Others squatted nearby, rolling out chapattis. Someone else was washing dishes at the pump. Then, one of the children decided it was time to bathe, so began sudsing up right there at the pump (a proper bath, of course, with underwear on). My point is, there were people everywhere. We were on the bed. Kids ran from room to room. Dogs, chickens and water buffalo right outside the front door. Pretty much your typical, chaotic family reunion, the high point of which was, appropriately, the food.

In his second letter to the Church in Corinth, Paul wrote, *We're not in charge of how you live out the faith, looking over your shoulders, suspiciously critical. We're partners, working alongside you, joyfully expectant. I know that you stand by your own faith, not ours"* (2 Cor 1:24, The Msg.). This is how we feel about Sanjay, John and their families. We're not in charge. They're not in charge. No one is the expert. They speak into our lives and we speak into theirs. Together, we humbly watch God do wonderful things, and, then wide-eyed, tell each other about it.

How can I be so happy about seeing you again soon, while at the same time feel so sad to be apart from them for so long?

Love,
Robin and all

1 July 2015
Dear Friends,

We've been back in Austin for one month. At times, we have felt like deer-caught-in-the-headlights. Thank you for the grace you've extended to us during these days of adjustment. Not that we're by any means fully adjusted (whatever that might mean), but shopping at the local grocery store isn't quite as intimidating as it was at first, and we're getting used to driving back on the other side of the road (note to self - driver must be in the middle of the road!).

Maybe because it's almost the Fourth and it's been three years since we celebrated on American soil, but the American value of independence is standing out to me these days. We Americans love people who pull themselves up by their own bootstraps. We are proud of our Abraham Lincolns, people who start with nothing, work hard and rise to the top. We encourage our children to be their own people. We applaud those who make their own way. We deride anyone who gets ahead by riding another's coattails.

I was reading this morning about the social dynamics of *patronage*.* It is a hallmark of Indian culture. India is a place of enormous social inequity. A very small number of people live at the top. The vast majority of people live with low status and low power. They struggle to survive. If they get sick, there's no money for and little understanding about medical help. Many (most?) of them are illiterate. Since they can't read, they don't know about government services which are available to help them. Their lives are bleak. There are few stories of anyone beating the odds or rising above his or her circumstances. Enter the Patron, the person with power, the privileged person at the top who is able to provide the goods and services that the vast majority desperately needs. In return, the people from the majority give honor and loyalty to the Patron.

Here in the West, and especially in America, we consider patronage unethical. We think it's unfair if someone gets a job or promotion on the basis of anything other than merit. We don't realize that for societies like India, patronage is not only the essential way to get ahead, it is expected and publicly acknowledged.

Our Indian brothers and sisters understand and value patronage. I do not. I proudly hum the Rocky theme song, even after the disaster which was Rocky V. The high value I place upon independence makes it hard for me to fully understand John 3:16. *For God so loved the world that He gave His only Son, that whoever believes in Him should not perish, but have eternal life*. People embroiled in the culture of patronage understand from this verse that God doesn't just love us. He is the most honored and magnificent Patron ever known.

The vast majority of Indians never try to pull themselves up by their own bootstraps. The ceiling is too rigid. We independent Americans are the one who believe we can "go west, young man," and improve our lives. Read through the eyes of patronage, John 3:16 reminds me that no matter how hard I pull on my bootstraps, I have nowhere to go. I am a part of the vast majority. My life is bleak. There is no escape. I am utterly at the mercy of the powers that be. But wait! God, my Patron, gives me protection and life. He rescues me, and so I have hope.

What is the proper response to The Patron of the world? Our Indian brothers and sisters can tell you - it's extreme gratitude, abandoned service and faithful obedience to the One who has lifted them up!

For Him, now in Texas for a while,
Robin, for us all
(*The Global Gospel: Achieving Missional World in our Multicultural World* by Werner Mischke.)

The following is an email conversation I had with a woman who wanted to know more about our work in India:

2 February 2016

Dear Robin,

...I am hesitant to follow your example in ministry for two reasons:

(1) Do the unsaved have spiritual understanding to explain the Word of God? You said that in Bible studies, you ask them to give input....I am wondering, if the Spirit leads us into all truth in His Word, can they hear Him, or are they just giving their opinions or using thinking from their carnal minds?

(2) I don't want to be limited by a method. I want people to be free to act on what the Holy Spirit might be telling a person to do or say in each unique situation.

Have you had either of these concerns? What is your response?......

Oh Friend, I'm glad you wrote! I have a statement, and then a question for you. First, a statement - you used the word "method" a few times in your email. Let me be clear - Steve and I do not follow or advocate any particular method of discipleship. Methods come and go. What we do is very simple - we teach people to listen to and then obey Jesus. That's it. Now, even as I write that, I know it's easy to say (and I used to say it, too), "That's what I try to do!" But, I have to tell you that even though I went to Bible college, no one taught me the importance of teaching others to listen to Jesus and do what He says. I knew how to create Bible study material. I knew how to preach a sermon. I knew how to teach. Frankly, I was pretty good. I wrote some cool studies. I was asked to speak at retreats and lead groups. I could argue the correct theological perspective for many of life's issues. But, I did not from a very early stage, train people to go straight to God, listen to Him, and then apply what He was saying to their lives.

Now, I have a question. Do you remember that old Sunday School song about the wise man and the foolish man? Without opening your Bible, do you remember the parable it's based on? This might sound weird, and no, I'm not being patronizing or trying to play games, but, do you remember it? Write me back. Tell me the parable. Don't look it up.

Dear Robin,

Was it the one about the wise man building his house upon the rock, and the foolish one on sand? When the winds came, the house on the Rock stood strong, but the other did not.

Thanks for being willing to answer my seemingly random question. Yes! It is a Sunday School song. Most of us know it, but it seems to have no point:

The wise man built his house upon the rock, house upon the rock,
house upon the rock. (2x)
And the rains came tumbling down!
The rains came down and the floods came up (x3)
And the house on the rock stood firm!
The foolish man built his house upon the sand, house upon the sand,
house upon the sand. (2x)
And the rains came tumbling down!
The rains came down and the floods came up (x3)
But the house on the sand felt flat!!

You can almost hear the Sunday School teacher saying, "Wasn't that fun, kids? Those hand motions are so fun! Now, let's all remember to be the wise man, not the foolish man."

Sadly, that's what most of us think, that the moral of the song is "Go, be wise," as if being wise is something we can do on our own. Or, maybe we don't even think about a possible moral. Maybe we just like the hand motions. We might rationalize that Jesus must be the Rock, so we should try to build our lives on Him instead of other things. But, what does that mean?

The passage upon which the song is based is a promise that Jesus made at the end of what we now call the Sermon on the Mount. Here's what He said:

Anyone who listens to my teaching and follows it is wise, like a person who builds a house on solid rock. Though the rain comes in torrents and the floodwaters rise and the winds beat against that house, it won't collapse because it is built on bedrock. But anyone who hears my teaching and doesn't_obey it is foolish, like a person who builds a house on sand. When the rains and floods come and the winds beat against that house, it will collapse with a mighty crash (Mt 7:24-27).

In your email, you asked a good question: *Do the unsaved have spiritual understanding to explain the Word of God in a discussion?*
Jesus answered your question. He promised that anyone who

listens to His teaching and follows it is wise, and will be like a person who builds his house on rock instead of sand. Foolish people build on sand. If we follow Jesus' teachings, we'll be as wise as the guy who builds on rock. Notice that Jesus didn't say those who already have His Spirit can listen and follow. He didn't say that those who have someone else interpret His teaching for them can listen and follow. He didn't say that only Jews could listen and follow, or only Christians. He said *anyone.*

My husband and I teach others, both those who call themselves followers of Christ and not, how to study the Bible with their families. Here is what the studies look like: First, the group reads a passage. Then, we ask the question, "What does this passage teach about God?" That's a different question from, "What do you think?" We don't ask people to share what they think the Word says. We ask them to share what it does say. Everyone in the group is expected to have their Bibles open and to be searching for what it says.

For example, let's pretend I'm not a follower of Jesus. I've never read the Bible before today, but here I am, now, reading the passage quoted above about the wise man. The question comes, "What does this passage teach about God?" First, I can see that God is able to make promises. Next, I see that God knows life is full of rain but He doesn't promise to stop it. I also see that His teaching isn't just something to just memorize or know in my head. His teaching is something I'm to apply to daily life, and when I do, He promises that my life won't fall apart when hard times come. Finally, I can see that I can choose to apply His teaching to my life or not. That's a whole lot of truth about God directly from His Word. No professional interpretations. No personal opinions. No Greek definitions. No commentaries. All I did was look at four verses with that one question in mind.

Can people who are not followers of Christ hear Him or understand His word? Jesus seemed to think that they could. It's also how it's always been. Every follower of Jesus you've ever met or read about was, at one point, a non-follower who heard His voice, listened and obeyed. Who was Abram? An uncircumcised Gentile living in an idolatrous nation who heard God speak. Who was Jacob? A grasping, selfish schemer who heard God speak. Who was Hagar? An Egyptian slave woman who wasn't part of God's covenant plan but heard God speak. Who was Paul? A murderous Pharisee who heard God speak, listened and obeyed. The truth is, all of us are exactly the person you described, including me. Including you.

To reiterate, my husband and I do not advocate a particular

method of ministry. We simply teach people to listen to Jesus by going right to His Word, and then doing what it says. Very early in our relationship with others, even before they call themselves His followers, we engage people with the Word and we ask them, "IF this story (or passage) were true, how would it affect your life this week?" If we hear a practical answer, then the next time we meet them, we ask how it went. It is amazing to see people applying God's truths to their lives, even before they call themselves His followers. Just as He's been doing for centuries now, God blesses their small acts of obedience or application. He doesn't wait for their theology to be perfect. Consider Abram again. When he first set out from Ur, he was being as obedient as he knew how to be, but he didn't have perfect theology. As soon as he got to the Promised Land and the rains stopped, he fled to Egypt and then allowed Sarai to get taken in by Pharaoh. God seemed OK with his less-than-perfect understanding. Time and again, God met with him, and along the way, Abram learned. And obeyed. Sometimes, He messed up, but at the end of his life, not only was Abram's faith bigger, but his understanding had grown, too. Thus, Abram (Abraham) became the example for all of us.

Learning along the way is still happening today. Take that hypothetical situation where I've just read my first Bible story. After studying the passage to find out what it teaches about God, the next question is, "Which of those truths has any impact in my life this week?" I'm pushed to think of a practical application. Jesus said that anyone can do that. Anyone can hear His teaching and follow it. Those who do will reap benefits, even in the very midst of life's storms.

It is possible that my husband and I talked about the Discovery Bible Study process so often that you got the impression that a tool is our passion. If so, forgive us. My husband and I are not "Discovery Bible Study Starters." We are disciple makers. Big difference.

Dear Robin,

Do the people who participate in this process, actually meet Him and become His followers?

You mention *meeting Him*. I'm wondering what you mean when you use that phrase. Most western Christians use that phrase to describe a process like this one: someone hears a sermon, mentally agrees, and at some point asks Jesus to come into his/her heart. The problem with this approach is there's very little- to-no Biblical basis for it. The whole believe-and-then-be-discipled approach is not what we see in

Scripture. It's not the pattern Jesus followed. Consider Peter. When did he meet God? Was it when...

- Jesus invited him to follow?
- Peter was baptizing people (John 4:2), even though at that point he hadn't even confessed Jesus as the Christ?
- Peter walked on the water?
- Peter confessed that Jesus was the Christ? Except, soon after that, Jesus rebuked him and called him *Satan*.
- Jesus restored him on the shore after His resurrection?
- Peter was filled with the Spirit at Pentecost?

Maybe Peter met God when he asked Jesus to come into his heart and forgive him of all his sins? Except, Peter never did that. None of the disciples prayed what we Americans call "the sinner's prayer." I can't find the prayer anywhere in Scripture.

When did Peter meet God? I think Peter met Him when he met Him, and that began his walk of faith. "But," some ask, "when was Peter *saved*?" And we argue and try to nitpick, and it never occurs to us that maybe we're asking an unnecessary question. Jesus did not demand faith before discipleship. He discipled people to faith.

Thank you for your honest questions.
Robin

7 October 2015
Dear Mom and Dad,

You gave us a wonderful furlough. Thank you. Your patience with us as we navigated the shock of re-entry was the balm to our open wounds. Now, here we are, back in our flat in Delhi. By Day 2, the kids were calling their friends and unpacking their rooms, already getting back into the swing of things. We look forward to seeing Sanjay later this week.

We joked often with you about Delhi dirt, noise and heat. Now that we're back, the heat really is stifling, dirt unconquerable, and the noise constant. But, honestly, who cares? They're unimportant in the light of what God is doing here. Testimonies continue to pour in from the churches about the God who can touch the unclean and make them clean, without Himself becoming defiled.

In most religions, including the one described in the book of Leviticus, the state of being clean or pure is a burden for humans carry. Our Hindu and Muslim neighbors are burdened by this daily struggle.

Remaining pure controls their every thought and action. Avoiding defilement overshadows their lives. They must greet others correctly, eat correctly, bathe correctly, even sleep correctly to remain pure. Certainly, they must avoid certain foods like pork and certain drinks like alcohol, but those decisions are easy to navigate. What's really burdensome for our neighbours is the daily, un-manageable stuff of life that also defiles. Illness. A woman's menstrual flow. Once defiled (and it is an issue of when, not if), our neighbours must make the proper restitution in order to be clean again.

One of the worst parts of having to maintain one's own purity is how isolating it is. Uncleanness is easy to catch. In the parable of the Good Samaritan, the priest and the scribe didn't touch the injured man. The impurity from his wounds would instantly pass to them if they touched him, even to help. How amazing, then, to read story after story of Jesus touching unclean people without becoming unclean. Lepers, the demon-possessed, a woman with an issue of blood, the dead, those who were ill - He touched them all without becoming defiled. Instead, He transferred His purity to them and made them clean! Amazing!*

Here in India, we're seeing God make unclean people clean. Just last week, 37 new disciples of Jesus took baptism in a state near to Delhi. Thank you for rejoicing with us (we can hear you from here). Please also pray for the countless others who are still enslaved by this need to maintain their own purity. God sent His Son so they could be free.

Back in India for Him, but missing you,
Robin, with Steve and the kids
(*The Global Gospel: Achieving Missional World in our Multicultural World by Werner Mischke)

1 November 2015
Dear Mom and Dad,

You are going to love the following story, especially in light of all you've heard over the years about caste divisions and oppressions.

There's a verse in the second chapter of Acts that says that the early church celebrated the Lord's Supper - *They worshiped together at the Temple each day, met in homes for the Lord's Supper, and shared their meals with great joy and generosity*. It came to light that while we were with you this past summer, a whole segment of the movement, involving many churches, were not taking the Lord's Supper. As Sanjay investigated, he learned that caste-ism was the problem. Casteism states that a high-caste person becomes spiritually unclean if he eats with a low-caste person. "We cannot take the Lord's Supper across caste lines," they told Sanjay. He didn't know how to tackle the issue, so he sent us an email asking, "What should we do?"

Teaching obedience is different from simply teaching about Jesus or about the Bible. Jesus' final command to His disciples was to teach others to obey. Racism in any form is unacceptable to God. Prejudice, having a preconceived notion about another human being, is anathema to the Gospel. Casteism is racism taken to the extreme. Caste teaches that, from birth, some people are better and more valuable than others. It is a huge issue. We needed to get this right. We needed a heart change on a core problem, not just verbal assent to a teaching.

Only the Lord can touch a heart. The churches needed to learn from the Bible, not us. We sent Sanjay a list of Bible verses which addressed casteism, the equality of all people in God's Kingdom, and who can take the Lord's Supper. We prayed. Sanjay took the Scriptures to the leaders. They studied God's Word together. They discussed what God was saying regarding casteism and the Lord's Supper. Sanjay did not preach or teach. He gave them the Scriptures. He prayed. He asked questions. They all looked at the verses together. Finally, the local leaders (not Sanjay) came to the conclusion that, "If I am in Jesus, I am no longer Brahmin. I can either be a Brahmin or in Jesus, but I cannot be both. If that's the option, then I want to be in Jesus!"

The leaders then did something we have seldom seen. They apologized. In front of each other, without attempting to save face or defend themselves, they admitted to Sanjay and their disciples, "I am sorry. I was wrong." After apologizing, the leaders intentionally gathered multiple churches from several different caste backgrounds, and all took communion together!

We are speechless. This is huge. As you know, casteism is the main filter through which the vast majority of Indians view relationships and community. God broke through their hearts and minds through His Word alone. Hebrews 12:4 says, *For the word of God is living and active and full of power [making it operative, energizing, and effective]. It is sharper than any two-edged sword, penetrating as far as the division of the soul and spirit [the completeness of a person], and of both joints and marrow [the deepest parts of our nature], exposing and judging the very thoughts and intentions of the heart* (AMP). This is truth we have always believed. Now, we have seen it in action. What joy!

Jesus commanded us to teach others to obey His commands

(Mt 28). Lecture, preaching and imparting theological doctrine have been the typical modes of instruction in the modern church. Best-sellers fly off of bookstore shelves or are downloaded in seconds onto our fancy phones. Yet, I wonder, are we teaching people to obey, or are we just teaching?

Simply awestruck,
Robin, with Steve, and the kids

14 December 2015
Dear Mom and Dad,
"I am a girl. I can't do anything." Doesn't that statement break your heart? Wish I could say that it's unusual. Below are quotes from a new, BBC-sponsored documentary called *India's Daughter*. Remember, these are not comments from a 50-year-old movie.

- "Boy and girl are not equal. Housework and housekeeping is for girls, not roaming in discos and bars at night doing wrong things, wearing wrong clothes."
- "About 20% girls are good."
- "Girl is far more responsible for rape than a boy."
- "In our society, we never allow girls to come out of the house after 6:30 or 7:30 or 8:30 with an unknown person" (*unknown* can refer to any non family member).
- "We have the best culture. In our culture, there's no place for a woman."

Recently, Sanjay and John were visiting some churches out in the villages. Most of the churches were families who became followers of Jesus during the past year. They were snake charmers. You have seen them. They sit near the Taj Mahal and other tourist sites, playing their flutes, coaxing cobras to rise out of baskets and "dance" to the music. Many of them worship the cobra, particularly because it's their main source of income. Several of these families are now following Jesus. Sanjay and John hadn't visited this area in several months. They were excited to be back. They couldn't wait to hear how the people were doing.

In the morning of the second day, Sanjay and John led a Bible study during which they shared several examples of normal, everyday people in Scripture who obeyed Jesus' command to make disciples. Some stories included women. Women were the first ones given the task of sharing the Good News of Jesus' resurrection. They supported

Jesus financially. At least one woman was in the Upper Room on the day of Pentecost. Philip had four (4!) daughters who prophesied. Lydia was a wealthy woman who hosted a church in her home. Sanjay and John wanted to impress upon these folks that this task of making disciples is for everyone. There is no male or female in Christ. The Samaritan woman is a perfect example of how this work is for all of us.

After the training was over, a young woman approached Sanjay and John. With tears pouring down her cheeks, she declared, "I am a girl. I can't do anything. At least, that's what I've always believed. Today, my prayers are answered. You showed me that God can use women. If those women could do it, I can do it, too. Now I know there is a place for me in Jesus' Kingdom."

As Sanjay and John prepared to return home, the people couldn't stop thanking them for coming. Why all the fuss? Apparently, visits from outsiders are rare. Infrequently, pastors from a nearby town visit, but they never stay long, and they never share a meal with the people because of their caste. Snake charmers are as low as Dalits. Yet, here were Sanjay and John staying in their homes, eating their food, drinking their water. Sanjay and John's visit gave the people dignity, but then, when they heard that even they, mere snake charmers, are invited to do the same work Jesus did (make disciples), they were astounded. Including the women!? Unbelievable! Life changing.

In the past eight months, in this one village, 68 families of the snake-charming caste and 19 families from other caste backgrounds have decided to follow Jesus. Most came to faith through the efforts of an illiterate (uneducated) young man.

Long ago, God chose an uneducated, teenage girl and her carpenter fiancée to be the parents of the most important Person who ever walked the earth. He hasn't changed. He still loves to work through the people we least expect (even me!) in the places we consider the most unlikely.

I love you, Mom and Dad. I'm sorry that we will be separated for yet another Christmas.

Love,
Robin, for us all

4 February 2016
Dear Mom and Dad,

In the last four years, we've seen more than 2,700 churches birthed and over 10,000 people take baptism. Whole families, and even villages are being changed. Women are no longer simple laborers in their homes, making food and serving chai, but are now free to meet with and pray for their neighbors who are being healed! Men are choosing life over drunkenness. They've stopped beating their wives, and are providing for their children. Parents are treasuring their daughters, not destroying them. You have a share in this abundant harvest.

In the midst of all this good news, there has been surprising personal upheaval. Since returning from our four months on the States, we have...

> ...missed Phoebe. In August, she did not receive a visa to return to India. She hopes to re-apply, but there is no way to know if she will be approved. Our partnership with the Indian nationals is priceless, but they don't live in Delhi. We see them only once or twice a month.
>
> ...realized that homeschooling is not a long-term option for our children. It was good and right to withdraw them from the Indian school system last spring, but homeschooling is not meeting all of their needs. Here in Delhi, homeschooling is truly *home* schooling. There are no co-ops, no One Day Academies. There's no yard to play in. No parks nearby. No local library. Additionally, we have learned recently that all of our closest expat friends will leave next year. Some will put a child in college and not return. Some are retiring. With our expat community disappearing soon and the friendships from the Indian school fading, the kids' world is becoming isolated.
>
> ...finally received long-sought information regarding taxes. Steve has asked questions about Indian taxes for over a decade. We have finally received unpleasant answers. We now understand that if we want to continue living in India, we will have to start paying 30% taxes here on our global income.
>
> ...seen that Sanjay and John don't need us. The work didn't stop during our absence. They don't need us. They never did.

We had no idea what to do about any of these issues, so asked the Lord for direction. Then, we waited. Watched. Prayed some more. Starting in November, a question began to echo in our minds - *What about moving to Penang, Malaysia?* There are many reasons:

- One of the best schools in the world for kids like ours is in Penang. They offer reduced rates for families like us who live on support.
- Malaysia is only a 4-hour flight from India. We will be able

to stay engaged with the work here in north India.

- Malaysia has the largest concentration of Indians anywhere in the world outside of India.
- English is spoken more widely in Malaysia than here in North India. We could definitely get around in normal daily life with English.
- The visa situation is more straightforward than in India.
- Taxes are easy. We'll pay in the States.
- Sanjay and John have blessed us, even commissioned us, to do whatever we need to do for our family. They will miss us, and hold us to the promise that a move doesn't mean a complete break, but we have their permission to go.
- Because of our experience here with Sanjay and John, people are starting to ask for our input. If the Lord is launching us into a type of coaching role around Asia, that will be easier to accomplish from outside India.

On Sunday the 31st, the whole family joined together in a time of listening prayer while reading through Ps 31 (the psalm for the day according to the American date format). By the end of the prayer time, we all were convinced that moving to Malaysia is the right thing, not only for the kids and their needs, but for ministry, as well. There we sat, finished with prayer and all pretty sure what the Lord was telling us to do, but none able to say it aloud. Finally, Aaron said, "I think we all know how God is leading, but we're afraid to say it."

Isa suggested that we say it in unison. She counted down from 3...2...1.. and then we all said, "We're moving to Malaysia" as we clapped and cheered. Big smiles. More cheering. We talked for a while, got used to the idea, and then did another countdown and said it again!

Throughout the day, the feeling of excitement remained. Even now, we're still reeling from the decision. Reality's setting in, too. Saying goodbye will be hard. Being newbies again will be hard. But, we feel great peace. Just this morning, I opened the computer to find yet another email from one of our prayer partners. She'd been praying for us and didn't know if these certain verses would mean anything to us, but she wanted to share them with us anyway. Of course, as you can imagine, they confirmed the decision to go.

We have lived in India for almost 12 years. We never pictured ourselves living anywhere else in Asia. Yet, the truth is, we have never just lived here. We have been/are on mission. The Lord of the Harvest is now directing us to make a change, and when He says, "It's time," the laborers say, "OK, Boss!"

Would you pray with us that our move to Malaysia will result in more fruit here in India? Maybe even in Malaysia, too. I look forward to sharing stories with you, every step of the way.

From India (for now),
Robin and Steve with the kids

16 February 2016
Hey Dad,

Thanks for sharing Mom with us. It's a joy to have her here!

Five years ago, soon after we became focused solely on disciple making, Steve heard the number *four* during a time of prayer. It was clear - we were to look for four national partners. We never wrote, *Our exit strategy is to have four national partners fully engaged in disciple making efforts*, but it became our prayer, "Lord, give us four!" Then we met Sanjay. "OK, Lord, one down. Three to go." For a while, we hoped that Suresh was #2, but in the end, he decided that growing the size of his own congregation was more important than releasing disciples to be church in their own areas. For years, then, we've prayed, "Lord, give us three more key leaders."

Three days ago, we met with two ladies who had heard of us through mutual friends. They wanted to learn more about the house churches. At one point during the conversation, Steve (engineer that he is) felt it important to explain that, no, there are not 3000 house churches in one stream of disciples. This many house churches were not birthed from Sanjay's efforts alone. He said, "There are actually four distinct streams of disciples," and then listed the names of the key leaders in the four streams.

Before this conversation, I had never heard Steve emphasize the leadership positions of these four men. He stressed Sanjay's involvement, how none of the streams would have started without him, but Steve was earnest about naming the other three names and designating those people as the heads of their disciple streams. I stared at him. Couldn't believe what I was hearing. I hadn't thought or prayed about the number four for a while. Here was Steve explaining that four partners is what we have.

When I mentioned it later to Steve, he was shocked, too. Hadn't made the connection. He was just trying to be honest about the nature of the work. We sat in silence. I finally said, "Hon, when people ask us why we're moving, we tend to mention the kids and their needs, visa issues and taxes. What if we're not leaving for any of those negative reasons, but because we're done, at least for now?"

It's a thought that still causes discomfort. Have we actually done what God wanted us to do? Really? How? When? To think that perhaps we've done all we were asked to do (for now) is astounding. We are speechless.

Four disciple making movements is a drop in the bucket here in this crowded subcontinent. God wants to do more. "Lord, give us ten!"

Love,
Robin, with Steve and the kids and Mom

How we will miss this place!

11 March 2016

Dear Mom and Dad,

Greetings from Delhi! It's strange to think that I won't be saying that for very much longer.

Sometimes, people ask if we're ever concerned about safety for ourselves or our partners, particularly because of the current, pro-Hindu government. They are usually surprised by our response, "Yes, the current government is radically pro-Hindu, but the house churches experience the most trouble from traditional Christians." Think about it, though. How many times did the Apostle Paul warn churches to be careful of the evil, Roman empire? Rather, time and again Paul warned churches to beware of legalists (Judiaizers), supposed fellow people of faith. We take great comfort from those verses. We feel like they were written just for us. What follows is an example of how modern Judiaizers regularly attempt to disrupt the movement.

Ravi is a simple man. He's from one of the lowest castes. He also has dark skin, which is looked down upon in Indian culture. Ravi became a follower of Jesus two years ago. He has never been to Bible college. He cannot read. Because Jesus changed him and blessed his life, Ravi shares the news of Jesus with others. He makes new disciples, baptizes them, and teaches them how to be the church. A few weeks ago, Ravi was at a river in north India baptizing a group of new disciples.

A traditional, paid pastor named Chayan was visiting the same village that day. He came to the river and disrupted the proceedings. "Get out of the water! Come here. Who gave you the right to baptize!? Are you a member of an official organization? You are not ordained. You should not be doing this." He was deeply offended that Ravi dared to baptise anyone.

Once Chayan quieted down, Ravi spoke, "You have been talking and talking. Now, it's my turn. Pastor, please look at Matthew 28." While Chayan looked up the passage, Ravi quoted verses 16-20 from memory. Someone standing nearby read the passage in a Hindi Bible. Chayan confirmed the Hindi passage with his English Bible. Ravi pointed out that Jesus did not merely suggest, but commanded His disciples to baptise, and this command was not limited ordained pastors or people affiliated with official organizations. Then, Ravi, the illiterate, "backward" farmer looked the important, city-dwelling, college-educated, salaried pastor in the face and said, "So, you go. You leave this place. If you stay, you will only continue speaking bad things, so you must go."

Chayan was speechless. And captivated. He couldn't bring himself to leave. He stuck around and watched the baptisms. When it was over, he told Ravi, "I need to know more about this. I have to know how you know these things." Ravi took Chayan to meet the man who had discipled him, another fellow lay-leader. Chayan was so amazed by all he heard that he went home and resigned his ministry position. Here are Chayan's own words:

> ...how many years I've been working with [that mission]. I came from Bible school [yet] this illiterate guy told me more than I knew in the Bible. Watching [him] do this baptism...his words were so wise and I am the fool. I've been to Bible school, and [my leaders] still won't let me baptise, only the bishop of our organization can baptize! [They] gave me a salary, but no authority [to actually do anything].

Chayan is now a fellow laborer in the movement. He's learning to walk in authority as Jesus' disciple, and to give that authority to others.

There was one other thing that fascinated Chayan about the baptisms that day. Ravi didn't charge for his services. Chayan had never seen free baptisms before. His organization charges people 2000Rs ($30usd) to be baptized (the equivalent of one month's income)!

Sanjay and John both worked for traditional ministries before meeting us. They verified that charging for baptisms is par-for-the-course in Christian ministry in north India.

God chooses the foolish things of the world to shame the wise. He chooses the weak things of the world to shame the strong (1 Corinthians 1:27). Please pray with us that God would raise up more fools in India who live out their authority in Jesus!

Much love,
Robin, for us all

19 April 2016

Dear Mom and Dad,

A few months ago, the leaders in some of the movement-churches began to wonder how they could help the young women in their area learn a trade. So many have no marketable skills and minimal-to-no education. How could the churches help? They decided to start a sewing centre, a common form of outreach among Christians in India. What makes this centre unique is that the churches did not ask us, the outsiders, for funds. They found a venue on their own. They hired a teacher. They purchased the materials. They are now training small batches of students for several months at a time.

The local church encouraged the Hindu teacher and students to include a Discovery Bible Study in their schedule. The church provided the tools they needed, but none of them came to lead it. Each day, the teacher and students studied one Bible story. They listened to a story on a speaker, and then asked each other simple questions such as "What does this story teach us about God?" and "What does this Bible story teach us about people?"

After weeks of studying a set of Bible stories that began with creation and ended with the resurrection, the teacher and eights students decided that they wanted to become followers of Jesus. Would the church baptise them? The church leaders were happy to oblige. A few days later, Sanjay called to tell me the good news that a Hindu teacher, five Hindu students and three Muslim students had all been baptised. Wasn't I excited?!

Mostly, I was confused. Single girls were baptised without their families? How? What did their families think? Were the girls now in danger? This testimony seemed to go against the pattern for outreach that Jesus used in Luke 10 when He instructed His disciples to reach households. From Noah in Genesis to the Philippian jailer in the book of Acts, there's a clear pattern of God saving whole families, not just individuals. Why had the local church disregarded the pattern? I responded to Sanjay's excitement with a less than optimistic, "What?!?!"

Then Sanjay told me the rest of the story. The girls' families not only gave permission for their daughters to be baptized, but they all attended the event and were so blessed by the experience that they are now asking if they, too, can be baptized! The teacher and the young ladies are now leading Discovery Studies in their own homes, discipling their families to faith.

We stand amazed. In this land where grandfathers reign supreme; where married women have no voice, much less single teenagers, a whole community of people not only supported their daughters when they made spiritual decisions on their own, but are now letting their daughters lead them in spiritual discussions in their homes. God's creativity puts our missiology and expert training manuals to shame. In John 6, Jesus stated that the Father is drawing people to Himself. The ways He chooses to do that are as varied as the people themselves.

From India for a little while longer,
Robin, for us all

17 May 2016

Dear Mom and Dad,

I love how God uses everyday things to teach us great truths. For instance, the Psalms tell us that God is a rock. Talk about ordinary. And valueless. A rock? Not a diamond. Not gold. A plain, old rock. We humans spend countless hours arguing theological terms but the Holy Spirit quietly uses ordinary, everyday things like seeds and rocks to reveal deep truths. He uses parenting, too.

Eirene realised a few months ago that she could graduate from high school one year early. Adjusting to this new reality has been a rollercoaster. I'm going to miss her more than words can say. At the same time, I know it's right and good that she begin the next phase of her life. She's ready. But, what if she's not ready? What if she makes a mistake? What if something unexpected happens? What if? Yet, this is what we've raised her for. Our job has been to parent her the best we could so that one day we'd see her thrive, independent from us. It's time for her to let go of our hands and grasp tightly to the hand of Jesus, and make her way in the world. Right? But, what if? Rollercoaster.

I haven't always applied what I know about parenting to disciple making. I haven't always recognized that my goal for my spiritual children is the same as with our actual children - to see them thrive with Jesus, independent of us. Usually, we who are in ministry hold onto our spiritual children for too long.

That we're leaving India next month still shocks us. Just months ago, we told people, "the longer we live in India, the longer we want to live in India." We now see that, just like we want more for Eirene than being dependent upon us all her life, God wants more for His Indian disciples than being dependent upon us. God knows, better than any of us do, that Sanjay and John and their spiritual children and grandchildren are not dependent upon us for the state of their spiritual lives. They are obeying Paul's injunction to *work out your own salvation with fear and trembling* (Phil 2:12). We must believe that God can direct them in that. Are Sanjay and John (and the others) ready? What if they aren't ready? What if they make mistakes? What if something bad happens? On the other hand, what if something good happens? We'll never know if we refuse to let them go. Why would we refuse? Only because, deep down, we don't really trust that God will lead them in the way they should go.

So, here we are, letting go of Eirene earlier than planned. I am so grateful that the One whose hand she will grasp is trustworthy. The same is true for our spiritual children. Those of us in leadership almost never think they're ready. Thankfully, God, the Rock, is always trust-worthy.

Loving you from India for a few more weeks,
Robin and Steve with the kids

P.S. Below are two recent testimonies from Sanjay and John. I have tried to stay as true to the original language as possible:

Praise the Lord! My name is Vishal. I reside in ___Village. One day Brother Ajab who lives [nearby] told me about Jesus and His work. After that [meeting], I attended house church [services]. He also gave me a speaker which had so many Bible stories on it. I brought it to my house. There is no one literate in my house. Every morning, I played the speaker and my mother [also listened] to the stories of the Bible. She came to know that Jesus is true and every-thing [else] is nonsense. She was an idol worshiper. She used to of-fer milk and water on the stones every morning [a typical mode of worship for devotees of Shiva], but after hearing all the stories she realized that she got nothing from these stones, and after that she also attended the house church along with me. Through [listening to the stories on] that speaker, my mother's life completely changed, in Jesus' name. Now she offers prayers [for others] and shares her testimony with others. Thanks to Jesus. Amen.

Praise the Lord! My name is Dev. I live in ___Village. My testimony is that after five years of marriage, yet I didn't have a child. I was living in a great agony. I went to many leaders (Hindu priests) who performed many rituals and sacrifices, but [nothing helped]. One day Brother Ajab came in our village and he asked me about my problem. I told him everything. He gave me a New Tes-tament and prayed for my wife. My wife and I prayed daily, and at-tended the house church worship services, and after one month she became pregnant. I became so happy and both of us took baptism in Jesus' name. Now my family is blessed in Jesus' name. Praise the Lord! Amen.

6 July 2016
Dear Mom and Dad,

I write to you today from Penang, Malaysia. Malaysia! This ad-venture in obedience never gets old.

On May 29, movers in Delhi packed 1/3 of our belongings. Two days later, we sold all that remained to a newly-arrived family in Delhi (May they be blessed and get good use of God's things!). Then, we moved into a friend's place for three weeks while the kids attended their annual summer camps up in the Himalayas.

June 22 was our departure. Sanjay, John and their families traveled the 4-hour trip (one-way) to say goodbye. We shared a meal, prayed together, and then wept. Uncontrollable, heart-wrenching sobs.

In Acts 20, we read about Paul's goodbye to his friends in Ephesus. Paul told them to *remember the three years I was with you...and then he entrusted them to God and His grace which he knew would be able to build them up. Finally, when he'd finished speaking, he knelt and prayed with them. They all cried as they embraced and kissed him good-bye....then they escorted him down to the ship*...(Acts 20:32-38). We now understand why they cried with Paul that day.

A couple of hours after our goodbyes to Sanjay and John, our closest personal friends came to say goodbye. We cried some more, hugged and prayed together. Then, they escorted us *down to the ship* (our taxis), and waved us off as we headed to Delhi International Airport. As we drove those familiar streets, we were overcome with the awareness of God's blessings. We lived in Delhi for 9 1/2 years, in India for a total of 12. Delhi is a hot, dirty, crowded, chaotic place, but we learned to love our lives there, to love the people, and to love what God is doing. We were (are!) so privileged.

And now, here we are. It's been 12 days. Life is peaceful on this tropical island. We can see the ocean from our temporary housing. We hope to move into our own flat in 2-3 weeks. Our new place is within walking distance of Isabel and Aaron's school, and should allow for an enjoyable lifestyle of walking and bicycling to markets and local restaurants. We will take Eirene to the college in Kuala Lumpur soon. It is almost time for another goodbye.

Steve is already planning his first trip to India. Great things are happening there because we left. The leaders have begun taking more ownership of the work. At their first meeting without us, they agreed that, though we will stay in touch, we are now gone. The work is theirs. They're praying together about how to see God's Kingdom expand even more. After all, 3000+ churches is great, but God wants to do more! He wants for no one to perish.

Eight weeks ago, Steve and I attended our last meeting with the church leaders in North India. They honored us with words of blessing, affirmation, and love, but the highest compliment they gave was this, "We have learned how important it is to listen to Jesus and simply obey whatever He tells us to do. And we know how important it is to teach others the same." Tears come to my eyes even now as I remember their words. When Jesus is Master of someone's life, when a person knows how to listen to Him and *to obey all His commands*, (Matt 28:20), there is nothing God can't do.

Thank you for loving us through yet another transition. We could not be on this journey without you.

All our love,
Robin, for us all, now in Penang!

June 2016 - November 2017

Fruit That Will Last
I no longer call you slaves...
Now you are my friends.
*I appointed you to **go***
*and produce **lasting** fruit.*
(John 15: 15-16)

5 August 2016

Dear Mom and Dad,

We left India almost two months ago. Eirene is now in college. Isabel and Aaron have started their new school. We have new phone numbers for the first time in ten years, and have exchanged Indian chai for various Malaysian styles of coffee. We also feel closer to what God is doing in India than ever.

Jesus' comment to His disciples echoes in our minds - *Let me say it again...It's better for you that I leave* (John 16:7, The Msg). How could the departure of the Word of God made flesh be better for them? Who did Jesus think He was kidding? His disciples didn't know it, but they needed Him to leave so that they could grow.

Grow they did. After Jesus went back to heaven, they healed the sick, raised the dead, were transported from one location to another, were imprisoned and stoned to death. They testified about God to high ranking government and religious leaders, they had disputes with each other, and loved each other. They prayed, had dreams and visions, spoke in other tongues, spread the Good News to new lands and new peoples, and made more disciples. In short, they did *greater things* than Jesus did, just as He said that they would.

If Jesus had stayed, the disciples' faith wouldn't have grown because there would have been no need. Jesus would have been right there, telling them what to do, or doing it for them. We're seeing the same thing in our small corner of the world. Jesus' disciples in India are stepping out in new ways because Brother Steve and Sister Robin left.

In the west, birth order no longer carries the same importance that it once did, back when only the eldest son could inherit the family land. Here in Asia, family relations and functions are still clearly defined. When our Indian friends call Steve *Big Brother*, they're not just being polite. It's his title and function.

During a recent phone call, Sanjay told us that soon after we left, the main leaders met together.

"Our big brother is now gone," they said. "The responsibility for this work has now fallen to us. We must ask God what He wants us to do." They prayed, and then made unified decisions:

- They organised the leadership by geographical areas, agreeing together who should be over what.
- They appointed sub-leaders.
- They decided, with transparency and in unity, how funds should be spent.
- They committed to weekly phone calls to stay connected with

each other.

These are unprecedented decisions. They are listening to the Lord together. God is doing amazing things in and through His Church in India!

Below are recent testimonies from the churches:

My name is Madhuri. I have suffered from fits for the past 5 years. Recently, I came to know about a house church in D. village. When I visited there, Brother S prayed for me. He gave me his number, and I called him after going home. For one week, he called faithfully and prayed for me over the phone. After that week of praying, I returned to the doctor. All medical reports were found to be normal. I was healed! I am illiterate, so am unable to read or write, but Brother S gave me a speaker with many Bible stories on it. I love to hear them, and my whole family and I are learning through listening. It is really amazing to learn the word of God so easily. There are five questions at the end of every story for discussion. The discussions are interesting and help us to know the stories well. With great joy, I can report that by using this speaker, I've been able to win two households for Jesus! There are 11 people in both houses. We have a great time meeting together and feel very blessed during the Bible study. I love my life in Christ. Thanks be to God! Amen.

My name is Shalini. My testimony is that I suffered from tuberculosis, but my family believed in black magic. They took me to a witch doctor who told them that I was possessed by an evil spirit. We spent huge amounts of money for him to heal me, but got nothing. I was in agony for almost three years. Then, one of my friends was going to a church meeting in K. village. I attended the worship service. Brother P and the whole church prayed for me. They also told me about God's Word and that power for healing is in the hand of Jesus. I put my faith in Jesus, and I was healed in Jesus' name! Brother P gave me a speaker that has many Bible stories on it. Now, my whole family and I listen daily to God's Word, and we also share the stories with others, too. Thanks to Jesus! Amen.

Praise the Lord! My name is Satya. I suffered from severe body pain and my wife was possessed by an evil spirit. Over time, I visited many doctors, and even witch doctors. I spent all my savings, but got nothing. One day, one of our neighbours saw me. I was crying. He asked me why. I told him everything. He told me about Jesus, and about a church that met in M. village. He gave me the contact number for Brother A. When I attended the service, Brother A and the whole church prayed for my wife and me. Brother A told us that if we believe in Jesus, He will do everything for us. After they prayed for us, both my wife and I felt so peaceful because we had been healed in Jesus' Name. Brother A then gave us a speaker with Bible stories on it. From that day, my wife, my whole family, and I are in Jesus. Every Friday, we host a prayer meeting for 20-30 people. I also share the Bible stories with others. There are 30-40 members of the church of which we are a part. All of us have memorized 4-5 Bible stories by listening to the speaker. We have shared these stories with many others, and some are very interested in learning more about Jesus. We go to their homes and talk. We give them God's Word. I hope that one day, they, too, will be good disciples of Jesus. Please pray for me, for my whole family, and for the church of which we are a part, that God will always give us the wisdom to reach more people in our community. Thanks to Jesus. Amen.

Rejoicing,
Robin, for us all

12 October 2016
Dear Mom and Dad,

Sorry that it's been over a month since I last wrote. The idea of writing an email about our new life here has been daunting. I haven't known what to share or how.

So, here I sit, typing at the desk in the bedroom of our new apartment, and I am, once again, simply awestruck by the view outside our window. Our room looks directly out at the sea, just 1/2 mile away. Any time of the day, we can look out the window of our bedroom or the living room, or we can sit on the balcony and just drink in the scene. The sea changes color constantly. Staring at it never gets old. But, if by chance we happen to look up at the clouds, we find ourselves mesmerised by those awesome things. One minute, they're high and huge, white and puffy; minutes later, they're low and gray and dropping buckets of rain. Who knew nature could be so captivating? We have never lived in a more beautiful place. Temperatures are relatively constant. It never gets hotter than the high 80s F, never cooler than the mid 70s. Steve tells me that *temperate* is the scientific word for all of this. All I know is that it's the opposite of Delhi. Nothing temperate about Delhi. Extreme is a better description, and not just for the temperatures.

- Delhi has an especially high average density of built-up area. At 19,600 people per sq. km, Delhi is twice as dense as both New York City and Tokyo. You know those movie scenes where the main character is walking amongst the crowds on the streets of New York? Delhi is twice that dense.
- Air pollution in Delhi is ten times higher than New York, London and Tokyo.*

Meanwhile, online travel guides routinely pick our new city as one of the Top Ten islands to visit in the world. Yahoo lists Penang as one of the Top Ten places to live in the whole world. In 2014, Lonely Planet declared that the best street food in all of Asia is made in Penang.** Given a choice, who wouldn't pick this ocean view over the litter-choked, sewer-smelling Yamuna River of Delhi? A person might even wonder, "Don't we wish we'd moved earlier?" And then I'm reminded of God's perspective:

> ...people are the consciousness of God in the world, the closest thing to Him in the physical realm, and a more vivid reminder than anything else in creation of His existence...If man really is fashioned...in the image of God, then clearly it follows that there is nothing on earth so near to God as a human being. The conclusion is inescapable, that to be in the presence of even the meanest, lowest, most repulsive specimen of humanity in the world is still to be closer to God than when looking...at a beautiful sunset..... Certainly, that is why there is nothing in the New Testament about beautiful sunsets. The heart of biblical theology is a man hanging on a cross, not a breathtaking scene from nature. For the Bible is centrally concerned with love....We cannot really love a sunset; we can only love a person....Similarly with hate: We cannot really despise anything in nature with anywhere near the vehemence with which we can despise and reject one another and the Lord our God.
> (*The Mystery of Marriage*, Mike Mason)

I know now that no view of the ocean, no afternoon spent watching clouds pass overhead, no glorious rainfall compares with the saving of a soul. Do I wish we'd left India earlier? Never. Steve and I wouldn't trade the fruit we've seen from among the lost for anything. *To be in the presence of even the meanest, lowest, most repulsive specimen of humanity in the world is still to be closer to God than when looking at a beautiful sunset.* The Son of Man came to seek and save the lost, not to sit on the edge of the Lake of Galilee and enjoy the view. Perhaps there were times when He did just that, but Jesus never forgot His purpose. Steve and I don't want to, either.

Please pray for us in these coming weeks. Pray that we don't grow weary in doing good (Gal 6:9). Pray that we keep the end in view (Rev 7:9-10). Finally, please don't stop praying for the peoples of crowded, polluted north India, that they will hear the Shepherd's voice and so, finally, be led to green pastures and peaceful waters (Ps 23).

We remain in Asia for Him, through you,
Robin for us all
(*https://lsecities.net/archives/key-statistics-on-delhi-from-urban-age-research/)
(**https://en.wikipedia.org/wiki/Penang)

8 February 2017

Dear Mom and Dad,

Steve and I visited India two weeks ago. It had been seven months since the move, the longest stretch of time I'd been out of India in ten years. Visiting Sanjay and John was wonderful, and surreal.

We cannot deny that life here is easier than Delhi, but we left our hearts in India with Sanjay and John and their families. We miss them, but we also know that God is in the middle of all these changes. There is nothing else to do but keep trusting God and moving forward. It helps that their reports continue to confirm it was time for us to leave. Current numbers put the movement at 7000 households in more than 935 villages.

Since 2012, at least 40,000 people have become followers of Jesus! They haven't simply added Jesus to their list of gods, but have thrown out their idols and officially chosen to worship Jesus, alone. These 7,000 (+/-) new families are forming churches which look very much like the churches in the first century. They spend their time *learning...sharing, breaking bread and praying together...they share...they give to those who have need...they are liked by [others]...* (Acts 2:42-47).

Thank you for every prayer you've prayed, every email you've written (and read), for visiting India and hosting us at "home." You have been our partners in this work, no matter the distance.

Many years ago, Jesus commanded us to make disciples (Mt 28:19). He also promised to build His church (Mt 16:18). You have stood with us every step of the way thus far. We have no idea what the next season holds for us, but of this we are sure - He is good at His job. He is building His church.

Your love and support have helped us play our very small part.

We love you!
Robin, for us all,

6 September 2017

Dear Mom and Dad,

We're busy here in Malaysia, but even now our hearts are still very much connected with the churches in India. We feel like we know what the Apostle Paul meant when he said,

> Every time we think of you, we thank God for you. Day and night you're in our prayers as we call to mind your...faith....love and....patience.....When the Message...came to you, it wasn't just words. Something happened in you. The Holy Spirit put steel in your convictions....Your lives are echoing the Master's Word...The news of your faith in God is out. We don't even have to say anything anymore - you're the message!...you deserted the dead idols of your old life so you could embrace and serve God, the true God... (1 Thess 1:5-10, The Message).

The following true story is typical of the reports we receive weekly about Indians who have *deserted the dead idols of their old life*:

> Greetings to you in the name of Jesus. My name is Sara. I live in GP village. One day, busy with housework at home, I heard a loud voice come through the open window. It seemed to come from my neighbour's house. The person was telling a story. I stopped to listen. It was an amazing story about how the world came to be. Back at the beginning, God made this world a beautiful place. Amazing! I had to give my full attention to that voice. Once the story was finished, I went to find out more about the story. Rini, my neighbour, told me that three months ago, she became a follower of Jesus. A man named Raj gave her an audio speaker with God's stories on it so she could learn what it means to follow Jesus. Rini now meets with 47 other people in her home each week to study the stories. They listen to a story, and then discuss questions about it. That creation story was so beautiful. I began to attend the meetings, and soon decided to also follow the God of those stories.
>
> One month later, I met Raj. He gave me a speaker, too,

and now we have two groups meeting in our village! Just like the group at Rini's house, we listen to a story, discuss what it teaches about God, and then try to apply it to our lives that week. We are all learning about God. I am very thankful to Raj for providing us with a speaker. Without it, we wouldn't be able to know this amazing and lovely God. I am an illiterate woman. I cannot read or write, but the stories on this speaker have changed my life. Thank you, Jesus!

Life in the subcontinent isn't easy. It is easy to become discouraged, to want to throw in the towel. Thankfully, God is not like us. He is not intimidated by evil. He loves the peoples of India. He is, literally, calling out to them through open windows in remote, backward villages. His disciples are also *echoing the Master's Word* in their lives. They are bold to speak about Him. They are bold with service. They are feeding the hungry, starting literacy centers for women, even pooling their meager incomes to buy medicine for those who can't afford it. They *are the Message*, and that is good news.

Love from us all, now in Malaysia but willing to go anywhere,
Robin, with Steve, Eirene, Isabel & Aaron

As of 2 November 2017, there are over 15,000 house churches in the movement in North India. Over 50,000 people have been baptised since 2012. How our God loves to save the lost!

We stand in awe of the fruit He has borne, but also know that He only wants to do more. After all, *the Lord does not delay [as though He were unable to act] and is not slow about His promise, as some count slowness, but is [extraordinarily] patient toward you, not wishing for any to perish but for all to come to repentance* (2 Peter 3:9, AMP).

May we never again be content with *some*. May God's desire for *all* be our vision, too.

28825586R00113

Made in the USA
Columbia, SC
17 October 2018